INTUITION IN THE DECISION-MAKING PROCESS AMONG AMERICAN AND BRAZILIAN BANKS LEADERS: A DELPHI STUDY

by

Karina Weil, D.M.

authorHOUSE®

AuthorHouse™
1663 Liberty Drive, Suite 200
Bloomington, IN 47403
www.authorhouse.com
Phone: 1-800-839-8640

First published by AuthorHouse   7/21/2008

ISBN: 978-1-4343-7906-1 (sc)

Printed in the United States of America
Bloomington, Indiana

This book is printed on acid-free paper.

ABSTRACT

Escalating geopolitical uncertainties, global inequities, partial financial analysis, and conventional rational approaches are factors that hinder bank leaders' accuracy in decision-making. To address this issue, this *Delphi* study intended to investigate the role of intuition in the decision-making process of international bank leaders. Employing a *multi-iterative computerized Delphi method, this* study *explored the perceptions of 33 American and Brazilian bank expert panelists regarding the phenomenon of intuition in their business decision-making. Data was collected across two rounds. Qualitative data analysis was accomplished by utilizing Atlas.Ti qualitative computer software. Quantitative data analysis followed the parameters of* descriptive statistics. *Five consensual themes emerged from the qualitative phase of this Delphi study: (a)* intuition is perceived as a feeling and a result of past experiences; (b) intuition in generic business and or personnel-related decision-making is significant; (c) intuition is minimal in the following ways: strategy formulation, determining cost reduction, performance gaps, and assessing market and political scenarios; (d) there is a growing relationship between intuition and logical and rational decision making; and (e) it behooves corporations to develop intuitive skills in their employees for enhanced decision-making. Statistical results indicated that the role of intuition in the overall reasoning process of both groups is prominent. Concerning financial decision-making, the role of intuition is minimal since both groups prefer to substantiate such decisions by numerical and factual data. American and Brazilian panelists agree on the increased connection between intuitive and rational thinking and the need for corporations to promote the development of intuitive abilities.

DEDICATION

I dedicate this dissertation to six people who have guided my journey. First, my beloved Guru, Sri Paramahansa Yogananda, whose invisible hand steered my will, reason and action in the right direction toward the highest good. Second, my cherished husband, Peter, whose embodiment of intuitive leadership, and unreserved complicity permeated the process of this dissertation. His generous outpourings of caring support and the timely and cheerful offerings of resources made all the difference, and for which I will be eternally and lovingly grateful. My adored son Andre, with his gift for deciphering problems adroitly, serenely and with the wittiest humor, was ever ready to devote countless hours to assist me with the intricacy and quandaries of statistical software. My treasured son Daniel, whose innate child-like faith in life, and ever-new interest in his mother's doings was always prepared to shout approval. These two extraordinary men symbolize my faith in the future of humanity. My much-loved mother, whom in her wisdom and intuition, envisioned, decades ago, the path I was to thread, and what I have become; and to my father, who would be able to value this accomplishment for what it entailed and for what it is worth. I wrote this dissertation imbued with the thought that it does not belong to me but to all whom it may benefit; now, and in the future.

ACKNOWLEDGEMENTS

While struggling to navigate through technical, and financial problems, changes in residence, delays, writer's blockages, and feelings of self-doubt that the writing of a dissertation inevitably brings, I could always count on my mentor Dr. Carolyn Salerno's zeal, and encouragement. Her unparalleled leadership skills and ability to raise my statistical and analytical mindset to higher and finer levels spurred me to broaden, and to re-elaborate my assumptions, thus saving me from making omissions. Such an extraordinary talent combined with a sincere, and impartial passion for the topic of intuition in decision-making was providential. One of the driving forces in a successful doctoral dissertation is the reliance on the faith and trust of a scholarly authority. As Dissertation Committee Members, Dr. Marilyn Simon and Dr. Anthony Poet were one such force. The unconditional friendship that was extended to me generously and in the spirit of service, at times unexpectedly, is a gift from God. It nurtured me and it brought a smile to my lips. Throughout the process of preparing for and writing the dissertation, I received the solidarity from such friends as Erik Fonseca – my brother –Dr. Richard Shuttler, Dr. Jack Sumner, Dr. Robert Drumm McNaughton, Mauro dos Santos, Cassio Gurjao, and all dear friends who, albeit not named, are of no less importance. God bless you all.

Table of Contents

List of Tables

List of Figures

CHAPTER 1: INTRODUCTION

Bank leaders have traditionally relied on numerical and statistical data to support financial decisions in uncertain and complex environments (Vaaler & McNamara, 2004). Vaill (1996) named this uncertain environment "the world of permanent white water" (p. iii). Bolman and Deal (1991) noted that to function in a highly volatile atmosphere, business leaders need to relinquish a propensity to assess problems through a single optic and adopt innovative and more powerful tools to deal with recurring or new challenges. The old scientific paradigm is not sufficient to deal with current problems (Arntz, Chasse & Vicente, 2005). Traditionally, leadership has favored rational thinking in decision-making (Capra, 1991; Khatri & Ng, 2000; Sadler-Smith & Shefy, 2004). Notwithstanding scientific evidence that intuition is a legitimate leadership tool in decision-making (Korac-Kakabadse, Kakabadse, &Kouzmin, 2002), intuitive knowledge is still disregarded in decision-making (Daake, Dawley, & Anthony, 2004). As a complement to analytical reasoning, intuition can provide an effective problem-solving and decision-making skill in situations obfuscated by ambiguity, instability, and information overload. The intent of this qualitative, *multi-iterative Delphi study* research study was to *explore, and conceptualize the phenomenon of intuition in the decision-making process among American and Brazilian bankers. Chapter 1 introduced the research by exploring the background, the problem, the purpose, the significance, the research questions, the nature, and the theoretical framework of the study.*

Background

This background section discusses the milieu surrounding the challenge of decision-making in the international banking industry in light of the current period of market and financial turbulence. This background section was organized by the following topics:(a) the management of profits and loses in an environment of unpredictable global complexities; (b) the mergers leading to financial losses; (c) the appropriateness of intuitive thinking in strategic decision-making; (d) the involvement of both rational and intuitive processes in decision-making; and (e) the role intuition plays in leadership.

Gherman (2002) observed that business leaders juggle uncertainty, and insufficient time to achieve rapid results, with the need to make sound and accurate decisions of capital importance in managing unpredictable global complexities. The assertion applies to bank leaders' credit or loan decisions. Table 1 depicts an approximate comparison of profits and allowances and loan provisions for losses among major U.S. and Brazilian banks. It also illustrates that credit decisions can lead to significant stipulations for credit loss, which in turn cause a decrease in banks' profitability. The information represented in Table 1 was a compilation of information gathered from annual reports and financial statements (Banco Central do Brasil, 2006; Banco Itaú Holding Financeira S.A., 2006; Bank of America, 2006; and Citibank, 2006). It contrasted the banks' total loans in 2006, total allowance or reserve, and the loan provisions against net profits. The total allowances and loan provisions banks make in order to protect their portfolio are high in comparison with the number of loans and the resulting net profit. Loan provisions are estimated expenditures a bank will have against each credit line that is extended to a client to protect themselves against losses. Loan allowances refer to reserves that increase as a loan reaches a level of non-performance. Although this capital allocation is mandatory and complies with the credit system risk-based evaluation, there are macro economic volatility variables beyond financial analysts' ability to predict change (Belkaoui, 2002). Specifically, "the macro-economic vulnerability of the small Mercosur countries to real devaluations in Brazil" (Catena, 2003, p.1) is a factor not to be taken for granted. Moreover, considering that developing countries (including Brazil) have a tarnished credit history (Catao & Kapur, 2006). Table 1 compares the amount of allowances, and provisions for loan losses with the resulting net profit.

Table 1

Banks Loan Provisions and Net Profit in US$ millions (as of 12/31/2006)

Bank	Total Loans	Loan Allowances	Loan Provisions	Net Profit
Banco Central do Brasil	61,160	3,952	3,320	2,827
Banco Itaú Holding	39,358	3,457	2,575	2,015
Bank of America	706,490	9,016	5,010	21,133
Citibank	679,192	8,940	6,738	17,046
TOTAL	1,486,200	25,365	17,643	43,021

In the example of Bank of America, the allowances and loan provisions for losses represent 60% of the net profit. Bank leaders argue that the percentage of allowances and loan provisions depicted above represent a high percentage of the net profits. If bank leaders can reduce the percentage of loan provisions, net profit will rise. Better decisions improve profit margins. In making the credit or loan decisions, as illustrated in Table 1, bank leaders rely on traditional factors of "demographics, application details and bureau data" (Slater, 2005, p.1). Nonetheless, such information does not eliminate loss risk. There are other issues that factor into the decision-making process over which bank leaders have no control. For example, environmental changes, wars, and cataclysms can affect the economic health and balance of several countries. Slater stated that the evolution of credit decision process is at "the cusp of change, where the advances in the science of credit risk assessment can be used beyond the risk decision" (p.1). Slater also emphasized that "every company is looking to its analytical and credit risk teams to make better decisions at each stage of the customer life cycle" (p.1). Dwight (2005) contended that while the objective is to ensure skillful competence in the financial markets, "asymmetric information" (p.1), among other issues, is a factor that can have a drastic effect on financial operations.

Beekie (2004) identified a positive relationship between emotional intelligence – of which intuition is a component – and the sales performance of financial advisors. This seems to indicate that the integration of an innovative factor in not only credit risk but also in general financial decisions might represent an available option to deal with the complexities of the financial environment.

Despite innovations in management research and the prominence attributed to rational decision-making and objective evaluations, "experts themselves may be prone to skewed decision-making as the stability of their own industry environment changes and their positioning in the industry shifts" (Vaaler & McNamara, 2004, p.1). Vaaler and McNamara noted the following comparisons between industry stability and industry turbulence: "expert credit-rating agencies and their risk ratings of emerging-market sovereign borrowers published from 1987 to 1998, a period that includes both industry stability (1987-1996) and industry turbulence set off by financial crises in several emerging-market countries (1997-1999)" (p.1). Khatri & Ng (2000) proposed the notion that environmental turbulence calls for an innovative decision-making approach. In support of this notion, Trailer & Morgan (2004) argued that among the reasons for relying on the virtues of intuition in decision-making include dealing with uncertainty and "an increased need for visionary thinking, inspired leadership and complex imagining" (p.1). Khatri, Ng, and Lee (2001) equated vision with charismatic leadership.

Bank leaders have prided themselves on financial modeling to support financial decisions. Albeit there is merit in this type of data, it is not infallible. The economic effects of the past Asian Financial Crisis confirmed its link to the poor quality of credit decisions that led to non-performing loans (Ahmad, 2002). Such decisions have lead to monumental financial losses of large-scale impact. The recent demise of global companies and other corporate scandals provide ample evidence to the limitations of the current decision-making process by leaders of major corporations (Watkins, 2004; Andrioff, 2005). To deal with the increasing conundrums of business complexities, leaders require the ability to incorporate constructs from different paradigms in order to move beyond the immediate reality onto subtler inner levels of consciousness (Garfield, Taylor, Dennis & Satzinger, 2001); an ability that intuitive thinkers possess. Such an achievement requires that executives combine intuition, logic and emotion to make fully informed decisions, and operate at their most effective levels (Hayashi, 2001), thus supporting Khatri & Ng's (2000) views that intuitive thinking is appropriate in strategic decision-making.

Further corroborating the perspective about intuitive framework in decision-making, Gladwell (2005), contended, "When experts make decisions, they don't logically and systematically compare available options. That is the way people are taught to make decisions, but in real life it is much too slow" (p.107). Some people evaluate a situation and "almost immediately act, drawing on experience and intuition" (p.107). Acting intuitively, revealed Gladwell, can be as effective as a decision arrived at in a deliberate, systematic fashion. Gladwell's assertions seem to cater to executives seeking the higher consciousness of instant cognition where saving time is essential (Halpern, 2005).

Khatri & Ng (2000), in a study about the role of intuition on strategic decision-making across the computer, banking, and utility industries, addressed the fact that one of the unquestioned assumptions embedded in management is that systematic analysis yields courses of action deemed superior to those stemming from intuitive processes. Tollefsen (2002) proposed, "This bias is largely motivated by the assumption that cognition is a process that takes place only within the individual mind/brain" (p.1). Griffin & Kahneman (2003) offered a competing perspective by stating, "The processes that produce brilliant intuitive insights are also the cause of systematic biases" (p.1). In view of this controversy, managers and leaders, typically pride themselves in favoring and employing rational thinking in their decision-making.

Nonetheless, Khatri & Ng's study found that intuition is an important component to decision-making and is positively associated with organizational performance. Similarly, in an article about the use of intuition on business ventures, Blotnicky (2002) started from the premise that intuition is not a sound way to make business decisions. Nonetheless, she agreed that intuition is a valuable tool in identifying environmental threats and opportunities. To that end, there seems to be an increasing need for an intuitional factor in the decision-making equation (Hayashi, 2001; Kay, 2002; Trailer & Morgan, 2004).

Familoni (2002), in a comparative study that investigated the role of intuition in the decision-making process of Nigerian and American executives, stated that intuition is a necessary leadership skill. The understanding of intuition becomes important–from a leadership standpoint–to the development of innovative and powerful strategic decision-making tools as organizations advance in the new millennium (Brockman & Simmonds, 1997; Gandossy & Sonnenfeld, 2004). Thus, it appears that intuition is a complementary source of knowledge to traditional logical reasoning (Faugier, 2005).

Despite the fact that the topic of intuition has received increased attention and has rapidly gained the status of a legitimate management tool in the decision-making process, managers generally still associate intuition with mystical issues (Khatri & Ng, 2000). Such a perception stems from regarding it as irrational (Patton, 2003). The reason for this irrational perception is that intuition lies on the threshold of the subconscious and other psychic factors (Khatri & Ng, 2000) and therefore, not immediately observable. Trailer & Morgan (2004) offered a parallel view by arguing that intuitive thinking is probabilistic at best. Trailer & Morgan's study revealed that the external validity of former research on intuition was "limited by the nature of uncertain events" (p.1) leading to inconsistency and failure. However, their findings also indicated that the dominant cause was individual lack of knowledge of intuition as well as a significant degree of variation in individual ability to use intuition. Such conclusions, combined with previous findings, fueled the motivation for further investigation. Therefore, the intent of this Delphi study research is to *investigate the influence of the phenomenon of intuition on decision-making among international bankers, specifically American and Brazilian bankers as it* relates to the reduction costs and performance improvement in the banking environment.

Problem Statement

The general problem was that decision makers in the banking industry face the constraints of increasing uncertainties, geopolitical risks, global imbalances and vulnerable financial outlook (Institute of International Finance Inc., 2005) when collecting financial data, and making decisions (see Table 1). The traditional analytical process of collecting financial data and making decisions does not take into account management's decision-making ability and management's ability to deal with various risks (Bank of America Annual Report, 2004). For example, the conventional use of financial ratio analysis to determine a company's financial performance has many weaknesses, including the effect of management's decisions on future performance (Gregoriou, Messier, & Sedzro, 2004).

The specific problem was that a lingering fixation on the use of the traditional analytical process poses obstacles to incorporate the use of intuition in decision-making (Dane & Pratt, 2004). Time and energy used in analytical processes are overly consumed (Familoni, 2002) to the detriment of decision-making that is time sensitive. Nonetheless, the use of intuition as a decision-making tool in [financial] organizations is yet to be accepted (Dane & Pratt, 2004).

The intent of this qualitative, multi-iterative Delphi research study was to investigate the phenomenon of intuition in the context of decision-making in the banking industry among 36 American and Brazilian bank leaders. The computerized multi-iteration Delphi method was relevant because it best described contemporary phenomena pertaining to real-life context and situations (Cleary, Packard, Armenakis, & Bederan, 1992).

Purpose of the Study

The purpose of this non-experimental, qualitative, multi-iterative Delphi study was to describe and conceptualize the phenomenon of intuition in the decision-making process of an expert panel of 36 American and Brazilian bank leaders. Convenience and snowball sampling strategies were utilized in the selection of the population. The study incorporated three rounds – two rounds of data collection and one round for presentation of the results. The rounds of data collection featured: (a) three open-ended questions; and (b) a Likert-type 5 point scale survey (Gall, Borg, & Gall, 2003; Leedy & Omrod, 2001) encompassing 20 questions, and were presented until consensus was achieved.

Given the fact that the bank panelists were geographically dispersed, the questions and survey were hosted online by utilizing a secure and professional online survey device (Zoomerang.com, 2006), a worldwide renowned online survey software. The Zoomerang concept to survey administration is an Internet-based survey tool that allows researchers to design, program, send, administer surveys, and analyze the results in real time. This approach was adequate because the process was minimally disruptive or invasive to the participants' daily routine. The data collection process followed a three-round format emblematic of the Delphi method of questions combined with summaries of responses that allowed the panelists to learn from others' responses. The essence of the Delphi method represented a unique approach to the problem in the way that it allowed access to attitudinal data not normally obtainable from other research activities (Lindstone & Turoff, 2002).

Analysis of data gathered from the open-ended questions was accomplished by using the Atlas.ti (Atlas.ti, 2006) qualitative data analysis software. The Atlas.ti (Atlas.ti, 2006) constituted the most recommended qualitative data analysis tool focusing on an interpretational, structural, and reflective analysis. Analysis of data gathered from the survey responses was performed by utilizing the Zoomerang.com (2006) online survey analysis capabilities. Zoomerang.com incorporated analysis tools that processed, tabulated, and yielded the percentages of the panelists' responses to the Likert-type scale survey items.

For the purpose of this research study, intuition was defined as an inherent faculty "which enables man to experience direct perception of truth without the intermediary of the senses"(Yogananda, 2003, p. 458). The metaphor of a direct communication with the cosmos is one present in the history of civilization from the thinking of the ancient philosophers to the musings of postmodern thinkers (Smith, 1995; Sowerby, 2001; Moser & van der Nat, 2003; McNaughton, 2003). Daniel Goleman (1998) called intuition the *inner rudder* (p.51) categorizing it as an important element of emotional intelligence. Recent research findings recognized intuition as a "gift from within, rather than a compilation of external experiences enhances the meaningfulness of intuition for leaders" (Church, 2005, p. iii).

Scientific investigations centering on intuition in management and leadership go back decades. Quoting Simon (1947), Wren (1994) proposed the definition of decision-making as a human choice and one of the executive functions comprised of two facets, analysis and synthesis. As Barnard (1942) described:

> Analysis, or the search for the 'strategic factors' that would create the set, or system of conditions necessary to accomplish the organization's purposes; and (b) synthesis, or the recognition of the interrelationships between elements or parts that together made up the whole system. (p. 271)

The multi-iterative Delphi method was an appropriate design for this study, because the contributions of the Delphi panel helped define reality by giving meaning to thoughts and beliefs (Linstone & Turoff, 2002). The use of a computerized Delphi survey enabled anonymous, systematic refinement of expert opinions with the aim of arriving at a combined or consensual position (Helmer, 1967; Simon 2006). The object of the Delphi method was to explore the views of a group of experts, in this case bank leaders, by giving them a series of questions and surveys interspersed with controlled opinion feedback (Helmer, 1967; Dalkey, 1969; Delbecq, 1975; Clayton, 1997; Linstone & Turoff, 2002). From this perspective, the Delphi method did not identify dependent, relationships or comparisons. The qualitative rationale was an appropriate method to this research study, because it rendered itself to the exploration and description of the use of intuition in the context of a *real life* situation. Based on the fact that the purpose of qualitative research is to describe, reveal, and verify findings in a *real world* setting (Leedy & Omrod, 2001), the use of intuition in decision-making occurring in a natural setting–the banking industry–was examined.

Significance of the Study

This section addressed the significance this Delphi study. Previous studies about intuition in decision-making were reviewed to ascertain the need for further investigation. The criteria used were: (a) lack of industry-specific research about intuitive decision-making in the banking industry; (b) possible industry-related differences among executives' use of intuitive decision-making in various industries; and (c) the perception of executives from various industries on the role of intuition in decision-making.

Khatri & Ng (2000), in a comparative study about the decision-making styles of executives across several industries including 158 banks, suggested executives in the banking industry tend to use significantly lower levels of intuitive thinking than do executives in the computer industry. Khatri & Ng indicated that research about intuition that focus on specific industries was needed in order to increase understanding and generalizability. Therefore, this research was significant for two reasons: (a) it represented the first industry-specific exploratory study on intuition in decision-making; and (b) it represented the first study investigating intuition among American and Brazilian bankers. As a study that further investigated the underlying reasons for the phenomenon of intuition, it was a significant undertaking for future studies and thought. Scientific advances in neurophysiology, the human psyche, and management behavior support the importance of subliminal intellectual activities, including intuition, in making choices. A deeper and broader understanding of intuition in decision-making can contribute to humanity's advancement of its higher abilities towards progress and fulfillment. Undertaking a research study that investigated the role and significance of intuition in decision-making was compelling.

Significance of the Study to Leadership

This section explained the reasons whereby this Delphi study on intuition in decision-making in the banking industry was potentially contributive to the existing body of leadership knowledge. As scientific data becomes insufficient, and complex variables mount (McNaughton, 2003), bank leaders' ability to make rapid, accurate and encompassing decisions necessitate a paradigm shift and groundbreaking approaches that might include intuition. Additionally, Familoni (2002) recommended that further studies be conducted to ascertain the degree to which intuition is developed in business leaders towards improved decision-making. In light of these facts, this study addressed three areas of significance to leadership. First, it examined decision-making processes in the context of the banking industry by exploring bank leaders' perception of intuition in decision-making.

Second, although the systematization of the decision-making process using scientific data gathering has contributed to improve organizational results (Latham &Vinyard, 2003), it does not provide complete information (English, 2004). Rather than discrediting the value of numerical data and factual reports in financial decision-making, this study explored what role intuition, as an additional or supplementary component, played in the decision-making of bank leaders.

Finally, past research has provided mixed evidence as to whether people compromise the quality of decisions by making decisions using intuitive thinking, or by using logical and rational deliberation (Liu, 2005). This study endeavored to elucidate the benefits bank leaders derive from using intuition in their decision-making as opposed to exclusively using logical reasoning. Moreover, Church (2005) noted, "Leaders who develop intuition realize greater skill in decision-making" (p.1). Expanding on Church's notion, Gladwell (2005) asserted that rational and intuitive thinking are neither good nor bad, but the intuitive thinking involves the ability to synthesize the whole. The iterative nature of this Delphi study helped bank leaders clarify the concept and definition, as well as the broader use of intuition in decision-making further expanding the understanding of this phenomenon.

The application of the Delphi design was significant to the bank leaders' participation in the study since it propitiated the assembly of a selected cadre of bank experts in a forum that was at once convenient, time and cost sensitive, and anonymous. Therefore, the selection of the Delphi design had a potential significance to leadership, because it allowed bank leaders to express their thoughts about a topic of importance to changing leadership paradigm in an informal setting. The rationale for this assertion derived from Familoni's (2002) opinion that intuition is at the core of innovative thinking and the needed shift in leadership paradigm.

Neglected for many centuries in the Western cultures, intuition is emerging as a desired competency. Intuition is resurging. The reason for this reawakened interest in intuition as an acceptable and respectable approach to decision-making stems from scientific evidence that intuition is a brain skill (Agor, 1986). In 1993, Yogananda (2003) noted that intuition is at the reach of any leader. McNaughton's (2003) concluded that leaders could expand intuition. The findings of Trailer & Morgan (2004) study suggested that individuals could develop intuition.

Leaders and managers have learned to make decisions in logical, sequential, linear, and exclusive ways. This approach to problem solving, however valid, has made decision makers too dependent on information authorities, facts and other externalities. In the process, they neglected to validate their innate inner wisdom. At the present, the imminent tribulations in the world's economic, environmental, and social-political scenarios require an encompassing, faster way to make decisions. The *immediate knowing*–expression coined by Sowerby (2001), or the *rapid cognition*–expression, (Gladwell, 2005), provided via intuition, as the counterpart to rational thinking, can lead to higher guidance and direction in finding solutions to problems.

From a technical and educational point of view, the consensual nature of the study, the distinctive characteristics of the banking industry, and the bank panelists' accrued learning on the topic of intuition in decision-making that resulted from the cumulative process of data collection combined with subsequent presentation of information, represented substantial differences from previous studies. In this regard, this Delphi study may have represented an original and significant contribution to the development of leadership decision-making paradigms from the point of view of the utilization of intuitive capabilities.

Nature of the Study

This section addressed the appropriateness of the qualitative method, and the appropriateness of the design, a *multi-iterative Delphi method,* to explore the phenomenon of intuition used in daily decision-making among individual American and Brazilian bank leaders. The selection of a qualitative approach for this study took in consideration the underlying principles of qualitative research in view of the nature of the topic and the population. Another determining reason for the selection of a qualitative approach was the exploratory characteristic of the study.

Qualitative studies are suitable for research on intuition in decision-making, because they take into consideration the multidimensional and subjective nature of this complex topic. Additionally, qualitative studies do not test hypothesis nor do they offer new theories. The purpose of qualitative studies is to describe the rationale of the specific phenomenon in its natural setting, interpret, gain insights, derive concepts, identify concerns, verify, findings in 'real world' settings, and validate the effectiveness of practices and beliefs (Leedy & Omrod, 2001). Simon (2006) noted that the qualitative paradigm is the ideal research approach when a thorough, comprehensive exploration about subjective, such as intuition, is the focus. Qualitative studies are the most adequate choice in order to maximize the learning about a topic before a theory can be developed (Gall, Borg & Gall, 2002).

Qualitative studies aim at gaining the most comprehensive and detailed view of a phenomenon, "drawing on personal reflections" (Creswell, 2002, p.58). The benefit that a qualitative method has over a quantitative approach is twofold: (a) it takes into account detailed and personal information from participants; and (b) it examines the topic or phenomenon externally, and in its internal structure. Quantitative methods test hypothesis and offer new theories. Qualitative studies are the most adequate choice in order to maximize the learning about a topic, before a theory can be developed (Gall, Borg & Gall, 2002). From these perspectives, the qualitative study research method was the most appropriate method for research on intuition and decision-making.

Qualitative researchers utilize multiple forms of data collection in their study, which may consist of observing or interviewing participants, documentation, electronic or note taking, and the use of analysis tools that can assist with getting the research question answered. Qualitative data collection is time consuming, and researchers may choose a structured manner to facilitate recording (Leedy & Omrod, 2001).

According to Smith (1995), the panel communication elicited in the Delphi obeys three criteria: "(a) anonymity; (b) iterations and controlled feedback; and (c) statistical group response" (p. 124). Fore these reasons, a *multi-iterative computer-based Delphi method seemed an appropriate design for this research study.* Since the chief concern of this study centered on anonymously ascertaining the perception and the use of intuitive practices that assisted bank leaders in improving decision-making, as they confront environmental complexities, the Delphi method was a suitable design for a research that has *futuristic overtones* (p.125). Using sequential rounds of inquiry, the Delphi method of data collection took into consideration the multidimensional nature of the complex topic of intuition.

The Delphi method is a research design that is predominantly qualitative in nature supported by descriptive "statistical analysis" (Topper, 2006, p. 4). Following Creswell (2002), Simon (2006) advanced that qualitative paradigm is the ideal research approach when a thorough, comprehensive investigation about subjective, such as intuition, is the focus. Thus, the value of a qualitative method utilizing the Delphi method as the research design lies in utilizing the panelists' perceptions and views for understanding of decision-making approaches (Simon, 2006).

According to Adler and Ziglio (1996), the Delphi method is a planned technique of data collection and refinement of knowledge obtained from assembled experts. The process entails a succession of questionnaires with controlled intermingled feedback. The four features that characterize the Delphi method, and distinguish it from other data collection designs, are: (a) a panel of geographically dispersed experts interact anonymously in a forum of discussion; (b) as the group interacts, the participants refine their views and increase their knowledge about the subject; (c) keeping track of participants' comments (Linstone & Turoff (2002); and (d) the presentation of statistical analysis (Olshfski & Joseph, 1991; Collins, Duschl, Millar, Osborne & Ratcliffe, 2001). Quoting Helmer (1983), Lang (1995) noted that the Delphi "relies on the informed intuitive opinions of specialists" (¶ 5). The circumstances that characterized this study reiterated those premises deeming the Delphi method as the appropriate research design. Firstly, there was the subjective nature of the topic of intuition in decision-making was not quantified, since it was based on subjective views. Secondly, the participants came from heterogeneous job positions. Thirdly, time and monetary considerations precluded the feasibility of meetings (Lindstone & Turoff, 2002). Finally, participants were considered as experts in their respective occupations.

Research Questions

Information gathered concerning the use of intuition in the decision-making of American and Brazilian bankers followed the Delphi design's systematic procedure of data collection. The research questions provided direction to the study and sought to *describe and conceptualize the phenomenon of using intuition in the decision-making process,* associated with reduced cost losses and performance gaps.

Two types of data collection guided the focus of this Delphi study: (a) three initial central open-ended questions that were asked at the beginning of the study, and (b) 20 5-point Likert-type survey items probed for more detail and required panelists to elaborate on the previous questions. The open-ended questions were broad in nature and preliminary "*intended to gather data*" [italics added] (Creswell, 2002, p. 154). The Likert-type scale survey questions were created based on the themes emerging from the responses to the open-ended questions and on the framework questions. The objective was to probe further on the panelists' responses to the open-ended questions and to obtain the majority of responses. The following 3 open-ended questions (Appendix E) and the subsequent 9 questions (Appendix F) respectively provided the framework for this study:

Framework for Open-ended Questions

Reflecting on your daily decision making activities:
1. How would you define intuition?
2. What role, if any, does intuition play in daily decision-making processes?
3. What role, if any, does intuition play in daily decision-making processes related to cost losses and performance gaps?

Framework for the development of the 5-point Likert-type survey.

1. How do American and Brazilian bank leaders define intuition?
2. What role does intuition play in the decision-making process of American and Brazilian bank leaders?

3. What are the views, beliefs, and attitudes of American and Brazilian ban leaders regarding the nature of intuition?

4. What benefits do American and Brazilian bank leaders gain from using intuition in decision-making as opposed to traditional fact-based decision-making?

5. How do American and Brazilian bank leaders describe their decision-making process?

6. In which decision-making business circumstances do American and Brazilian bank leaders prefer to rely on intuition?

7. What are the American and Brazilian bank leaders' experiences of the impact of intuition on decision-making on cost reduction and performance?

8. What are the American and Brazilian bank leaders' perceptions of the interrelationship between intuition and decision-making?

9. What are the American and Brazilian bank leaders' beliefs about the development of intuition in banking corporations?

According to Creswell (2002), procedural subsequent questions indicate the possible next steps in analyzing the data in the study. Though there was a general notion of the steps that would be taken later in analyzing the data, some latitude was allowed for the questions and themes to evolve and refine during the course of the study "because the procedures for a qualitative study will evolve and shift and cannot be identified early in a study" (p.153).

Theoretical Framework

The theoretical underpinnings that guided this qualitative, multi-iterative Delphi research study involved an understanding of the philosophies that support the evolution of decision-making in organizational management, the implications that the evolution of decision-making has to leadership, and the role that intuition plays in decision-making in several industries. Such rationale was grounded on the beliefs emerging from the following research: (a) Khatri & Ng (2000) noted that intuition does not denote a phenomenon contrary to reason, but rather, an observable fact that rests outside the province of reason; (b) intuition is associated with organizational effectiveness (Andersen, 2000); (c) intuition is not an antithesis to analytic decision-making, but a phenomenon inherently post analytic (Goldberg, 2005); (d) the numerous variables, as well as, the increasing uncertainties posed by the complexities of the global financial market, require that leaders develop the ability to have a holistic perception of a situation; and (d) postmodern leadership is steering away from traditional leadership styles towards one that employs diverse sources of knowledge (Familoni, 2002).

Examination of the history of management decision-making reveals that "rational analysis, systematic empiricism, representationalism and causal determinism" (Chia, 2001, p. 1) are the four epistemological that underpin the foundations of organizational management. Chia further stated that while the creation of management thought would not be possible had not it been for the utilization of systematic and linear reasoning, the world is confronting "a new realm of reality in which wisdom, knowledge and information, can no longer be simply understood" (p. 24) in codified terms. "Instead, the instability and 'noise', informational fluxes, dispersions, and transient configurations of relations are what characterize the phantom-like qualities of our post-modern world" (p.24). To deal with post-modern ambiguity, integrated and encompassing modes of understanding must break the limitations of those of a purely explicit, logic and well-defined nature, concluded Chia.

Corroborating this view, Kopeikina (2006) affirmed that when leaders the making of good decisions involve reaching a clarity of mind that has been described in neurophysiology studies as "a balance of physical, mental and emotional systems" (p.3). Kopeikina further stated that effective leaders "define the rightness of a decision by the degree to which it is aligned with their vision" (p.3). "Analytical methods do not constitute vision" (p.5) maintained Kopeikina, because "vision is the product of intuition" (p.5).

In a similar vein, Khatri & Ng (2000) considered the rational model of decision-making to be the central reason for the obstacles that the United States organizations faced in competing with foreign companies in the 1970s and 1980s. Following Mintzberg (1994), Khatri & Ng concluded that the expression 'strategic planning' is an oxymoron. Mintzberg (1994) contended that business leaders cannot plan strategy since planning entails analysis and strategy is a result of synthesis.

Lloyd and Mori (2002) echoed Mintzberg's ideas by asserting that an over reliance on factual data in strategic decision-making has not protected organizations from errors and oversights. Moreover, purely logical approaches to decision-making have dire limitations. In the views of Boyd, Gupta, and Sussman (2001), strategy formulation is of necessity a creative feat, purport, of which intuition constitutes an indispensable ingredient.

To this date, the debate is still raging. The pervading notion that confines intuitive decision-making to the realm of the metaphysical or irrational results is the belief that intuitive processes are outside the boundaries of scientific study, said Khatri and Ng (2000). Nonetheless, the latest advances in cognitive science and artificial intelligence suggested that intuitive thinking is a legitimate cognitive function, and therefore, are neither irrational nor paranormal, emphasized Khatri and Ng. Theoretical evidence from neurophysiology and neurobiology studies demonstrated that the right brain hemisphere rules the unknown and the unexplored, while the left-brain hemisphere is a repository of vast prior analytic experience. In other words, the left hemisphere stores analysis compressed and crystallized and the right hemisphere visualizes. The left-brain hemisphere is the product of analytic processes that are compacted to such an extent and intensity that its internal structure may not be entirely obvious (Goldberg, 2005). When an expert uses intuitive thinking in decision-making, the left-brain circumvents the orderly, logical, procedural steps because it had already registered and condensed the extensive use of such procedures in the past (Goldberg). According to Goldberg, this phenomenon is synonymous with intuition. Neurophysiology discoveries in the last two decades appear to be influencing the way business leaders approach decision-making, which may pave the way to the much-needed shift in paradigm and innovative thinking, said Goldberg.

In the face of unpredictability and turbulence, as demonstrated by the catastrophes in Thailand, Indonesia, Sri Lanka and New Orleans, "one of the failings of typical strategic planning approaches: their minimization and disregard of intuition in the strategic planning process" (Boyd, Gupta & Sussman, 2001, p.1). With the resulting economic and mental strain comes the leadership necessity of a proportionate level of agility in making decisions and the ability to respond to crises. In a study that investigated the effects of, and the relationships between the risk and uncertainty on capital investments, Alessandri (2002) found that:

> Under perceptions of greater uncertainty, firms tended to employ decision processes that relied upon intuition and experience rather than analysis. Furthermore, perceptions of greater uncertainty were associated with the pursuit of alternatives that sought acceptable–rather than optimal–solutions. In contrast, under perceptions of greater risk, the opposite relationship exists–firms tended to employ more extensive analysis to find the optimal investment decision. (p.1)

One source or manifestation of such knowledge is the "inner voice of intuition" (p.19).

Jeffrey Mishlove (1994), when interviewing business leaders in an international symposium on intuition in the business world, discovered that the most serious problems affecting business leaders are the physical and emotional stress resulting from the lack of time and control over the variables in order to make quick decisions of high impact on the organization's productivity, and image. The ability to make quick, broadly accepted and high quality decisions consistently in a fast-moving environment is the foundation of sound leadership (Vaill, 1996; Patton, 2003; Cartwright, 2004). However, guidance on adopting a holistic process in decision-making seems to be scarce. In that regard, Patton (2003) stated that:

Approaches typically proposed by management gurus tend to advocate performing careful analyses rather than trusting intuition or deciding issues with a combination of rational analysis and intuition because analyses are insufficient. However, in order to make good decisions when constrained by time and uncertainty, slogans and analytical tricks are no substitute for good intuition. (p.3)

Echoing Patton's view, Bolton (2005) contended that leaders must "be able to trust his or her own intuition which is based upon true self-confidence" (p.1). Such competencies constitute some of the differentiators among professionals. Bolton's ideas converge with those proposed by the military. "Brilliant military leadership is a result of intuition" (Tal, 2004, p.1). Using the Israeli war of 1948 as an example, Tal described how its generals placed their intuition above traditional military education in winning the battles. Bakken & Gilljam (2003) make a strong case about the importance of intuition in military command.

Definitions

The terms employed in this study stemmed from the review of literature. The terms include: (a) intuition; (b) views; (c) beliefs; (d) attitudes; (e) Delphi method; (f) decision-making; (g) leadership); (h) management; (i) cost reductions; (j) performance gaps; and (l) panel of experts. For clarity purposes, the definitions of the terms adopted in this study follow according to the order in which they appeared.

Intuition. Henry Bergson (1992), who produced some of the seminal philosophical and psychological discussions about the meaning of intuition, proposed that intuition is the apprehension of the entire process, a discovery of truth, and a revelation of the real world. Bergson described it as emerging from profound layers of the human mind, being a phenomenon that is different from the usual intellectual functions. Khatri & Ng (2000) stated that intuition synthesizes isolated bits of data and experiences into an integrated picture.

For the purpose of this Delphi study, intuition was defined as "a global and instantaneous comprehension of an object, truth, or fact" (Chaui, 2003, p.45). This description was fitting since rational activity includes "intuitive reasoning" (p.45). Intuitus, in Latin, means to see directly without proofs or demonstrations, said Chaui. Five discipline fields—emotions, neuroscience, and evolutionary psychology, organizational leadership and cognitive science—are currently researching the fundaments of intuition and investigating the mechanisms of decision-making. With distinct literature, set of concepts, and generalizations, these disciplines seem to base their assumptions on two premises: (a) intuition is an activity that takes place in the right brain hemisphere activity; and (b) intuition is the accumulation of vast amounts of information and experiences that crystallize into habit that then promotes recognition of situation patterns. While the there is wide acceptance to the scientific evidence of right brain hemisphere activity, there is a limit on an individual's long-term memory access said Patton (2003).

As Patton (2003) pointed out, it is important to distinguish two different usages of the word intuition. Generally, the term appears in ordinary speech to denote unconscious sporadic and vague glimpses of information, feelings, and inspirations. Since there seem to have neither logical, causal relationship nor connection with external stimuli, they are frequently dismissed as mere "lucky guesses, creative flashes, insights at best, and at worst, just irrational concoctions of the, unconscious mind" (p.3).

Findings from neurophysiologic research accept the view that intuition is an unpredictable but integrated process that occurs in the human nervous system (Kopeikina, 2006). Nonetheless, traditional management and academic scholars appear to rely on the belief that logic and intuition are two different things. Conservative scholars see the latter as a subjective, unreliable, unscientific, and lacking in substantial evidence (Bloxham & Borge, 2006). However, views regarding intuition as the true source of wisdom are emerging in the scientific literature (Cooper & Sawaf, 1997; Fisher, 1999; Familoni, 2002; Patton, 2003; Yogananda, 2003; McNaughton, 2003). Another view places this definition in association with the realm of feelings and the irrational (Nassar, 2006). Despite this controversy, the idea that endures is that intuition, as an "intrinsic value" (Anderson, 2005, p.1) "implies the possibility of an unerring accuracy and appropriateness—a connection with an awareness that flows through the underlying deep connectivity of things and events" (Patton, 2003, p. 4). In a hermeneutic, phenomenological study (Church, 2005), six themes emerged as definitions of intuition: (a) intuition is a compilation of experiences; (b) intuition is secretive; (c) intuition is a gift from within; and (d) meaningfulness in life emerge for leaders who integrate intuition in decision-making.

Views. Views are opinions, sight and points of view (The Cambridge Dictionary Online, 2005). The vernacular employs the word as a particular manner of considering or contemplating a subject matter with reference to action. Views also describe an aim, an intention, purpose, prospect, contemplation, judgment, estimation assessment, impression valuation or expectation on a given matter. The Merriam-Webster Dictionary of the Encyclopedia Britannica Online (2006) presents "1. Extant or range of vision: sight" as synonymous with view. It also notes "2. The act of seeing or examining: inspection" (¶ 1). Views are further defined as "the ability to see something or to be seen from a particular position" (AskOxford.com, 2006, ¶ 1). Views also appeared as "a way of regarding something" (¶ 1). As it relates to the topic under study, views on intuition refer to a general account, conception or description of intuition, which may lead to a theory.

Belief. Belief was defined in the AskOxford.com (2006) as "a firmly held opinion" (¶ 1); "a feeling that something exists or is true" (¶ 1). Accordingly, a belief displays confidence of truth or existence of a fact, idea, or concept that may not be immediately susceptible to rigorous and meticulous proof (AskOxford, 2006). Beliefs in intuition encompass faith, and trust without concrete evidence (AskOxford, 2006). Nonaka and Takeuchi (1995) equated personal beliefs with tacit knowledge.

Attitudes. Attitudes qualify a subjective, multifarious, and intricate mental state involving beliefs, feelings, values and dispositions to act in certain ways (Webster's Online Dictionary, 2001). Collins & Smith (2004) identified new standards of attitude "as being fully committed, and that which the company understands" (p.1). Hillson and Murray-Webster (2004) applied the term attitude to refer to "internal human mental processes and positioning ...to chosen responses to situations" (p.3).

Delphi method. Adler & Ziglio (1996) defined The Delphi method as a technique that gleans information pertinent to the topic under investigation for decision-making purposes. Expanding on Adler and Ziglio's views, Simon (2006) described the Delphi modus operandi as a controlled process of gathering information from specialists, authorities, or connoisseurs, by means of a string of questionnaires whose responses are analyzed individually before the next is administered or introduced. Furthermore, other variations of the Delphi process also represent a forum of communication and exchange of ideas among a group of experts, which promotes homogenous consent of views and opinions (Helmer, 1977; Linstone & Turoff, 2002).

Decision-making. Decision-making is a personal choice (Wren, 1994); and as one of the executive functions comprised of two facets, that Wren described as:

> Analysis, or the search for the 'strategic factors' that would create the set...of conditions necessary to accomplish the organization's purposes; and (b) synthesis, or the recognition of the interrelationships between elements or parts that together made up the whole system. (p. 271)

In summary, decision-making pertains to a resolution in which the judgment about a fact, idea, act, and or concept is formally pronounced. Decision-making entails the act of making up one's mind by defining goals, determining problem triggers, setting requirements and choosing a course of action. Making decisions is a central aspect of leadership (Khatri & Ng, 2000).

Leadership. One of the most classical and widely accepted definitions of leadership comes from Bass (1990) who stated that leadership is:

The focus of group processes, as a matter of personality... of inducing compliance, as the exercise of influence..., as a form of persuasion, as a power relation, as an instrument to achieve goals, as an effect of interaction, as a differentiated role, as initiation of structure, and as many combinations of these definitions. (p.11)

Harrison (1999) steered the discussion toward the need to draw some lessons from this myriad of theories by proposing that leadership is about a liaison, a rapport between individuals connected by a shared goal (p.7). Harrison (1999) implied that leadership is a conscious act, which is not intimidating and moral. Harrison (1999) concluded that, the new leadership paradigm for the new century would have to incorporate the issues of the interdependence and collaboration, and the ineffectiveness of dominium, and restraint.

Post industrial organizational relationships and advances in leadership research brought about increased refinement of the understanding of the behaviors and characteristics of leaders. To mirror these nuances, the notions of leadership fall under five modalities: (a) autocratic leadership; (b) transactional leadership; (c) transformational leadership; (d) servant leadership; and (e) level five leadership. Autocratic leadership entails "the use of commands and is becoming obsolete in today's world" (Weiskittel, 1999, p.1). Transactional leadership has elements of autocratic leadership in its rewards and punishment relationships between leaders and followers. Specifically, transactional leadership involves an exchange of task and reward (Burns, 1978). Transformational leadership differs from transactional in that it bespeaks of a capacity to foster fundamental change, and create new paradigms fueled by values of a higher order, and an inspirational and visionary orientation (Banerji & Krishnan, 2000). Greenleaf (2002) defined servant leadership in the following manner:

> [It] is a practical philosophy that supports people who choose to serve first, and then lead as a way of expanding service to individuals and institutions. Servant-leaders may or may not hold formal leadership positions. Servant-leadership encourages collaboration, trust, foresight, listening, and the ethical use of power and empowerment (¶ 1).

Level 5 leadership incorporates elements of servant leadership in a paradoxical combination of "triumph of humility and fierce resolve" (Collins, 2001, p.1) to take a company from a merely good one to a grand one without pretense and without seeking credit for oneself. Instead, Level 5 leaders assign credit to their followers.

Contemporary views of leadership touch on the spiritual (Graber, 2001). Similarly, Houston and Sokolow's (2006) who suggested that leadership is a state of enlightenment that rests upon wisdom. Another perspective comes from Tubbs and Schulz's (2006) whose perceptions of leadership include the following notions:

Inspiring others, going against outdated or ineffective practices, building trust, varying leadership to the demands of the situation, delegating effectively, evaluating others, mentoring others, leading with sensitivity and empathy, seeing nuances of alternatives, not just either/or extremes, and serving as an appropriate role model for others. (p.2)

Management. "The terms management and leadership are often used interchangeably" (McLean, 2005, p.1), equating one to the other. However, the two concepts do not intertwine. McLean (2005) described management as control and manipulation; characterizing leadership as the ability to influence and persuade. The act of managing pertains to administering by means of rational methods and procedures.

Cost reductions. Cost reduction is benchmarking streamlining exercise utilized in organizations to increase effectiveness in performance and competitiveness. Cost reduction practices identify areas of higher expenditures than the competition, advance potential savings measures "such as reducing the number of suppliers or making better use of technology" (Law & Owe, 1999, ¶ 4).

Performance gaps. Coop (2006) defines performance as "achieving objectives by control" (p.1). A gap or discrepancy or ample divergence in performance refers to a decrease in quality and productivity. For the purposes of this study, performance gap will be regarded as a company's inability to achieve "profit margin, return on assets, return on equity, and return on sales [as] the key indicators for the measure of financial performance" (Chang, Chang & Hsin, 2006, p.3).

Panel of experts. Xu and Gutierrez (2006) established that a panel of experts is an assembled group of professionals who has significant knowledge and understanding about a specific area. The panel of experts is invited to opine on a number of "issues and scenarios gleaned from the literature review" (p.1). The selection of experts is a crucial element in the Delphi method. According to Rodriguez et al. (2003) experts require "recognized expertise" (p.2). The experts for this study will be limited to American and Brazilian bankers, for the reason that they represent the leaders of their organizations and they possess the skills, experience and knowledge that sustain banking operations. Research studies using the Delphi method require individuals who have knowledge of the topic being investigated who are defined as a panel of well-versed individuals; hence the designation experts (Hasson et al., 2000). Olshfski and Joseph (1991) defined expert according to "credentials and experience" (p. 298). Mullen (2003) offered the most comprehensive definition about an expert being any person who can provide a pertinent input.

Assumptions

This Delphi study entailed a cross-cultural view of two nationalities. Substantial knowledge and understanding of the American and Brazilian cultures' language, norms, practices and customs reasonably safeguarded the survey against potential errors in procedure and interpretation (Neuman, 1997). There was awareness of the potential of courtesy bias and it was addressed in the limitation section of the study. The choice of cultures included in the survey were made "on both substantive (e.g., theoretical, research question) and practical grounds" (p.407). Although at each phase of the research, sampling, data collection, and interviewing were conducted with strict observation to language codes and social customs, the Brazilian panelists were fluent in the English language and acclimatized to the American culture. This factor contributed to an equal treatment of the two groups.

Scope

This section pays particular attention to the conditions that constituted the boundaries of the Delphi study. Several of these conditions included: (a) the definition of the study population; (b) the nationalities represented in the population; (c) the geographic location of the population; and (d) the recruiting and selection technique. Parameters were imposed prior to the inception of the study in order to provide a sharp focus. Delimitations and restrictions were used to narrow the scope of the study. Limitations are an intrinsic factor in all research studies (Cooper and Schindler, 2003). An elaboration of the four conditions afore mentioned was provided below.

The target population sample comprised 36 leaders from American and Brazilian multinational banks. Because the expert panelists came from a wide geographic area on the globe, geographic quotas did not apply. Moreover, no emphasis was placed on gender proportion in the analysis of data since the purpose of the study did not depend on this criterion. Additionally, since the selection process relied on the panelists' reputation in the banking community and on nomination, a priori information regarding gender was not available. Therefore, no predictions were made as to how gender differences would bear on the panelists' responses.

The operational definition of the population sample encompassed bank executives in leadership positions across a variety of job functions such as credit directors, marketing directors, traders, stockbrokers, CEOS, and investment bankers, all of whom represented a cross-section of banking occupations in the two geographical areas and cultures. From a statistical point of view, the multiplicity of job positions increased the chance of generalizability of results. A combination of stratified, quota, and snowball sampling constituted the selection methods utilized.

Random sampling was not a pre-requisite of the Delphi method (Schmidt, 1995); for this reason, prospective panelists derived from a pool of personal contacts in Brazil, in the United States and in South East Asia, and consequently by nomination and personal reference. Convenience and snowballing sampling were employed because these methods amplify the statistic probability requirements (Neuman, 1997). The core advantage of convenience and snowball sampling methods was its inherent referral system, which increased the population sample size and quality. These sampling techniques were effective in both cultures. Snowball sampling was the most culturally effective in the Brazilian social cultural environment owing to the fact that Brazilians were more likely to participate knowing that an acquaintance had referred them. Reputation among colleagues may have been a determining factor in the participation since the banking community in Brazil is tightly connected which heightens the bank leaders' visibility.

Limitations

Seven limitations circumscribed this Delphi study, namely: (a) participants; (b) instruments; (c) generalizability; (d) objectivity; (e) external validity; (f) attrition; and (g) nature of the Delphi method. Further discussion on the dimensions of the study limitations ensued as follows:

Participants. This study was limited to subjects who agree to participate voluntarily. Advancement to subsequent rounds was limited to those bankers that participated in the previous iteration.

Instruments. The validity of this study was limited to the reliability of the instruments used. The instruments included a set of open-ended questions and a Likert-type scale survey. This study did not utilize previously developed questions and surveys.

Generalizability. Generalization of the results to other situations may have been limited (Leedy & Omrod, 2001). A strategy to mitigate this problem will be to replicate the study with different populations, organizations, and industries.

Objectivity. An anticipated limitation has to do with researcher integrity and lack of trust (Neuman, 1997). The problem in question is the tendency to impose views on the participants. This can compromise objectivity of the findings owing to partiality and predisposition toward intuition as a decision-making skill prior to starting the study. Positivist research states that perceptions, impressions, and biases have no place in research and the detachment, neutrality and objectivity will lead to empirical confirmation of the truth of a phenomenon, affirmed Neuman.

The challenge in this study was one of remaining objective and unbiased given that, "there are many opportunities for a researcher's personal influence to affect qualitative research" (p. 332). On the other hand, Neuman presupposed that is unfeasible to abolish the influence of subjectivity entirely. The reason for that is that qualitative research involves the study of human elements and their subjective views and attitudes in a natural setting that is closer to real life situations. Therefore, an unequivocal stance was adopted in the study and before the public based on Neuman's explanations of the kind of ethical conduct researchers must assume:

> Recognizing the human factor does not mean that a qualitative researcher arbitrarily interjects personal opinions or selects evidence to support personal prejudices. Instead, a researcher's presence is always an explicit issue. A qualitative researcher takes advantage of personal insight, feelings, and perspective as a human being to understand the social life under study, but is aware of his or her values or assumptions. He or she takes measures to guard against the influence of prior beliefs or assumptions when doing research. Rather than hiding behind 'objective' techniques, the qualitative researcher is forthright and makes his or her values explicit in a report. Qualitative researchers tell readers how they gathered data and how they see the evidence. (p. 334)

External validity. Threats to external validity constituted another limitation to this study. Neuman identified three types of inherent limitations to external validity: (a) the population type and attrition; (b) the location; and (c) the period. An elaboration of the issues follows below.

Population type. Although the participants belonged in an interconnected network, there was no direct link among them. The effective use of the theory of proximal similarity ensured homogeneity among the participants. This feature was discussed in the delimitations section. The population size was statistically representative according to the Delphi method standards.

Attrition. Retention was a concern over which there was little or no control. The participants were limited to the volunteers who completed the interview and survey questions posted on-line. Although a significant demand on the panelists' in terms of their commitment to time and participation was not anticipated, work pressures faced by the panelists' hindered optimal participation in the study time span. To encourage participation and commitment, a strategy for reward was developed. In an informal survey among bankers, a symbolic incentive in the form of a gift certificate from a reputed French computer store (FENAC) was deemed appropriate for the population and the effort involved. In this manner, it was expected that any eventual degree of attrition and possible response degradation might diminish. Nevertheless, the panelists expressed lack of interest in receiving any form of incentive on the grounds of altruism.

Delphi method. Since its inception, the Delphi method of data collection has evolved into other types, namely, the Policy Delphi, and the computer-enabled Delphi or Modified Delphi (Rockwell, Furgason, & Marx, 2000; Lindstone and Turoff, 2002). The study procedures entailed the utilization of the computerized Delphi since this version was the most suited to research involving geographically dispersed panelists.

Delimitations

This Delphi study confined itself to surveying American and Brazilian bankers, focusing on the role of intuition in decision-making. Only Native Americans and Brazilians were invited for the study. The population, the location, and the time applying to the investigation of intuition constituted the essence and the boundaries of this study. Accordingly, the issues of internal and external validity and generalizability are further elaborated in this section. These do not represent a disclaimer but the parameters by means of which the findings may be credible and generalized.

Following the characteristics of a predominantly qualitative study (Simon, 2006), this investigation was less tightly controlled and predictable than an experimental study. Consequently, it may theoretically have a higher degree of external validity and generalizability, which constituted the study goal. As discussed in the limitations section of this proposal, a delicate balance between external and internal validity may be attained by a combination of well-thought-out design and sampling strategies.

American and Brazilian bank leaders circumscribed the population delimitation for this research as this investigative study proposed to explore the decision-making styles of bank leaders in both cultural settings. A sub-section of the population delimitation was the degree of similarity among the participants. Besides being bank executives, the bank leaders who participated in this study had careers in banking, were incumbents of a banking position during the study, worked employees at a banking institution, and were in a leadership position with strategic and financial decisions accountabilities. Location delimitations did not apply to this study. Since the study was conducted on-line, panelists were at their respective offices during the data collection phases. The three phases of data collection, data summarization and presentation, and final report lasted for a period of approximately two months.

Chapter Summary

Chapter 1 identified the research problem and addressed the important concern with the role of intuition in the decision-making process of American and Brazilian bankers. The source of the problem stemmed from the literature reviews and views obtained from experts in the banking industry. The research problem demonstrated the need to advance knowledge in the area of decision-making addressing the reasons to improve understanding of this important leadership tool in organizations. The problem and the nature of the study established the rationale for the selection of the most suitable data collection procedures. An introduction and explanation of the Delphi method as the selected design for this study followed. The data collection components of the Delphi method included an initial set of open-ended questions and a Likert-type scale survey. In addition, this chapter introduced the purpose of the qualitative method and Delphi design research based on the historical and theoretical background of the decision-making problem currently affecting American and Brazilian banks in the light of their present attitude toward intuition as a decision-making tool.

Definitions for the specific terms frequently employed in the research study in relation to the topic of intuition contained: (a) intuition; (b) views; (c) beliefs; (d) attitudes; (e) Delphi method ; (f) decision-making; (g) leadership; (h) management; (i) cost reductions; (j) performance gap; and (k) panel of experts. Seeking to remove ambiguities and ensure clarity, the chapter examined studies conducted about the views, beliefs, prejudices and attitudes, surrounding the phenomenon of intuition. Khatri and Ng's (2000) comparison among several industries, including the banking industry, was particularly relevant. The significance of the study to the current body of organizational leadership knowledge and the potential benefits to the panelists was discussed.

Assumptions are those aspects of a study that "often remain hidden or unstated" (Neuman, 2000, p.41) Therefore, in order to deepen the understanding of the concepts related to this research study, the assumptions supporting these concepts were identified. The underlying critical assumptions of the study entailed cultural sensitivity and the ability to deal with the cross-cultural nature of the population. This chapter also established the boundaries demarcating the study by describing the scope, limitations and delimitations. The discussion was supported by a review of literature presented in the next chapter.

CHAPTER 2: LITERATURE REVIEW

This chapter provides an assessment of literary works about intuition covering a time span of over five decades. The chapter also presents a description of the criteria utilized in the search process for the pertinent material as well as a list of the works researched. All literary sources are of scholarly, professional and scientific class. The different types of texts were searched adopting headings and titles as a search method to retrieve articles, journals, and dissertations. The literature review centers on three main themes, namely: (a) a historical overview; (b) the phenomenon of intuition as seen by philosophy, psychology, brain research, management, and the spiritual scriptures; (c) leadership decision-making styles; and (d) an outlook of the banking industry and a description of the general population of bankers.

A preliminary literature review revealed that, although the topic of intuition is rapidly ceasing to be equated with the paranormal phenomena to gain the place status of a legitimate tool utilized by leaders in the decision-making process (Korac-Kakabadse, Kakabadse, & Kouzmin, 2002), it still is generally discounted and spurned (Sadler-Smith & Shefy, 2004). For the most part, leaders typically pride themselves in favoring and employing rational thinking in decision-making (Capra, 1990; Khatri & Ng 2000; Sadler-Smith & Shefy 2004). Dane and Pratt (2004) contended that regardless of the reasons behind this preference, leaders still confront the conundrum posed by having to respond quickly, qualitatively, and effectively to market pressures and the lack of time-consuming formalized decision-making processes. Sadler-Smith and Shefy put forth the following argument:

> Recent scientific discoveries about human cognition, coupled with dissatisfaction with the limitations imposed by rational thinking, have led to a resurgence of interest on intuition. In order to cope with new levels of complexity and decision-making, actors will not just need knowledge but meaningful knowledge or, in Aristotelian terms, wisdom. (p.1)

Church (2005) contended, "The integration of all the resources a leader has is the intelligent, responsible choice" (p. 95). Fractional and inadequate decision-making is a likely phenomenon during industry and environmental turbulence leading to substandard bank performance (Khatri & Ng, 2000; Huges, Lang, Mester, Moon & Pagano, 2002; McNamara & Vaaler, 2004; Dane & Pratt, 2004). Present leaders today are under immense pressure, having to contend with ambiguity, instability and uncertainty resulting from accelerated change, and information overload; and could benefit from the aid of intuition, and the wisdom that comes with it, to be capable of leading and making the right business choices for their organization and their employees (Fischer, 1999; Khatri & Ng, 2000).

Dane and Pratt (2004) stated that the increasing volume of research looking to intuition as a viable management tool in the life cycle of corporate high-risk decision-making is still scanty. This situation is further aggravated by two factors: (a) a dearth in studies that focus on intuition in specific industries (Khatri & Ng, 2000); and (b) in Dane and Pratt's view, an enduring propensity in management literature to convey muddled definitions of intuition. The review of the literature seeks to clarify and distinguish the various definitions of intuition. The following section presents the literature search criteria rationale for the topics afore discussed.

Title Searches

The scope of the literature reviewed comprises EBSCOhost, and ProQuest databases from the University of Phoenix Online Library as primary sources of books, dissertations and articles. Two hundred and fifty sources were reviewed and 231 were considered in this proposal. A break down of the literary sources is as follows: (a) 26 books on classical and post modern philosophy; (c) 12 books on various subjects addressing the topic of intuition; (c) 14 books and 62 articles on management; (d) 17 research books and 29 articles; and (e) 39 articles, 8 dissertations on the theme of intuition, and 3 dissertations on international finance conducted within the last five years. Additionally, 25 articles addressing financial topics were examined (see Table 2). Supplementary related sources from the internet search engines Google, and Microsoft Internet Explorer were searched.

In keeping with the topic of this study, twenty words and phrases were employed as heading and title searches to retrieve pertinent literature: (a) intuition; (b) intuition and global management; (c) intuition and decision-making; (d) tacit knowledge; (e) intuition vs. rational reasoning; (f) intuition and leadership; (g) intuition and management; (h) intuition and organizations; (i) intuitive management; (j) banking decisions; (k) global leadership and intuition; (l) intuition in business; (m) intuition and psychology; (n) intuition and psychology; (o) intuition and global competencies; (p) intuition and Emotional Intelligence; (q) Delphi study; (r) credit decision; (s) credit risk; and (t) international finance.

Articles

In accordance with the requirements and standards stipulated, the core articles considered for this literature review derived from accredited scholars and researchers were peer-reviewed and attained from academic and/or management journals. Otherwise, articles originated from the management practice. Articles were reviewed and categorized according to the degree of relevance to the topic. Approximately 32 articles chiefly centered on intuition. However, the predominance of the articles focused on intuition in the context of leadership decision-making. Articles that studied intuition in various disciplines including education, psychology, neurophysiology, engineering and nursing, also applied. Ancillary articles that alluded to intuition in the context of spirituality in leadership and in the work place, as well as studies that discussed viewpoints contrary to the perspective of this study were also examined.

Research Documents

Documents reviewed included 14 cross-disciplinary dissertations that addressed the concept of intuition in leadership decision-making, as well as the current state of the international financial environment. They are presented in this chapter. Eight recent studies date from the last five years and represent the following institutions: University of Akron; Texas A& M University; University of Phoenix; Institute of Transpersonal Psychology; Fielding Graduate Institute; University of Oregon; University of California; Nova Southeastern University; The Ohio State University; and The University of Saint Thomas.

Books that explored the use of intuition in decision-making included the following authors: Agor (1968, 1985, and 1990); Parikh (1994); Goleman (1996; 1998); and Gladwell (2005). Books that explored the concept of intuition included the following authors: Maslow (1968); Jung (1973); Anderson (1990); Capra (1990); Zukav (1991); Bergson (1992); Parikh (1994); Vaill (1996); Cooper and Sawaf (1996); Reale (1997); Goleman (1998); Duhot (1999); Hessen (1999); Werner & Pluhar (1999); Baldini (2000); Philippe (2002); Baggini and Stangroom (2003); Griffin and Kahneman (2003); Moser and vander Nat (2003); Yogananda (2003); Chauí, (2003); Aranha and Martins (2005);Arntz, Chasse and Vicente (2005); Homer & Westcott (2005); Medina and Wood (2005); Reale (2005); and Zingano (2005). Credit extension and analysis reports about the performance of the banking industry in the United States and in Brazil were obtained from Standard & Poor's (2005) – the world's premier supplier of information on investment research and credit indices (www.standardandpoors.com, 2005)– and from the Bank of America, Banco Central do Brasil, Banco Itaú, and Citibank annual reports.

Journals Researched

Journals researched represented a wide range of disciplines, namely education, postmodernism, psychology, managerial psychology, marketing, systems and technology, nursing, finance, and engineering. National and international journals present in this chapter applied to this review. The categories of journals reviewed included management and leadership science, organizational, medical, financial, philosophy, metaphysics and organizational psychology journals. The intent was to glean a multiple perspective on the topic of intuition from various sectors. The majority of the journals selected for this review of literature fall under the category of scholarly and peer-reviewed. Exception was made to professional or industry journals as they contain current information on the practice. Table 2 depicts a categorized view of the materials considered for the literature review dating from 1888 through to 2006.

Table 2

1888-2006 Literature

Category	Scholarly Books	Empirical Research & Dissertations	Scholarly Reviewed Articles in Journal and Periodicals	Founding Theorists	Total
Intuition	4	1	25	3	33
Intuition and Decision-making	2	3	22	2	29
Intuition and Leadership	2	5	39	5	51
Intuition-EQ	3	1	1	1	86
International Banking	-	*3*	*25*	-	*28*
Philosophy	9	-	3	1	13
Psychology	3	1	11	1	16
Intuition and Brain Research	1	-	4	-	5
Dictionary	8	-	-		8
Delphi Research	17	1	29	4	51
Totals	50	15	159	17	240

Historical Overview

The main purpose of this section is to summarize in chronological order the genesis of discussions about intuition in the Eastern and Western civilizations. The second objective is to glean an understanding about the phenomenon of intuition from multidisciplinary perspectives. The third task is to examine discussions about intuition in leadership and management research.

The historical origins of the debates about intuition can be traced back to man's early cogitations in the quest for truth and knowledge in the light of the activities of the human psyche (Chauí, 2003); and, in that sense, cannot be separated from the history of Eastern and Western philosophies (McNaughton, 2003). At this intersection, history becomes the history of philosophy. Nonetheless, the differences between Eastern and Western philosophies are obvious (Lewis, 2002).

The evolution of Western thought occurred under the premise that the acquisition of knowledge occurs via empirical means, thus giving full weight to the rational mind as separated from nature or the world. In accordance with Lewis (2002), the concept of objective knowledge "is inherently Western in origin" (¶ 3). Eastern thought, on the other hand, emphasizes the "inner subjective realities" (Schmidt, 1995, p. 16).

The philosophy of the East contrasts with the Western mode of an objective reality by proposing the existence of a reality beyond the material sphere. Schmidt (1995) described it as a belief system that views the world in the way it filters through the five senses as "essentially an illusory world that is solely a manifestation of thought forms and subject to the winds of consciousness" (p.17). For example the decision-making of North Americans is guided by "promotion-focused information and Chinese people are persuaded more by prevention-focused information" (Briley & Aaker, 2006). From the beginning, intuition has fascinated philosophers, researchers and business theorists (Schmidt, 1995). The fascination with the topic of intuition stems from the fact that researchers and theorists acknowledge the limitations of human reasoning and attention span to effective problem solving and decision-making (Patton, 2003). In the quest to acquire the capability of making accurate decisions, intuition has been the object of much research and debate. Yet, a thorough comprehension and applicability of intuition are still hampered by misconceptions, misconstruction, and reasoning fallacies. Understanding the phenomenon of intuition entails the analysis of philosophical, psychological, cognitive, neurophysiologic, and emotional factors (Kopeikina, 2006).

The Greek philosophers' incursions on intuition maintained the possibility to access the ultimate standard by means of which one can apprehend reality (Aranha & Martins,

2005). The ancient philosophical truths may be equally applicable in a postmodern world where a "crisis in paradigm" (p.90) and information overload may hinder precision in decision-making. The postmodern philosophical underpinnings of such findings surfaced with Walter Truet Anderson who proposed that different groups of people construct different realities; in the same way dissimilar languages represent different approaches to experiencing life. Anderson stated that perceptions of reality are human constructions. However, the internal dialogues in the physical mind create distractions that trap the observation of reality (Yogananda, 2003).

From a cognitive point of view, intuition is a subjective process that does not depend on thought since it is not subject to the logical and analytical mental process but rather, transcends it (Jung, 1973). To intuitively understand or know something precludes the rationalization process. Psychologist Carl Jung (1973) stated that the term intuition does not denote anything contrary to reason; however, intuition represents something that lies outside the domains of reason. Gladwell (2005) offered comparable views arguing that a considerable amount of human cognitive processes fall under the domain of the unconscious. Such an assertion put in check previous assumptions that information processing and assimilation yield to conscious mechanisms (Bargh & Chartrand, 1999). Offering a similar perspective, Khatri & Ng (2000), quoting Agor (1990), affirmed that humans' actions succumb to a subconscious storage of information than via the conscious activities of the physical mind.

Such discussions do not demerit the value of rational analysis. Khatri and Ng (2000) conceded that rational thinking is a "useful and indispensable tool" (p. 4) in decision-making. In fact, experience plays an important role in decision-making. It creates pathways in the brain, cognitive template (or schema) against which new information contrast, affirmed Halpern (2005).

Leonard, Beauvais, and Scholl (2005) offered a different perspective in describing rational analysis as a cognitive style characteristic of individuals who make decisions based on logical and factual connections, whereas intuitive thinking is characteristic of individuals who see the big picture, grasp abstract concepts, and establish relationships and values. These differences determine a person's decision-making style (Leonard, Beauvais & Scholl, 2005), and therefore, must be taken into consideration in the development of a decision-making theory (Khatri & Ng, 2000).

From a management point of view, the emphasis placed by leaders and scholars on rational decision-making, as a superior approach over intuitive decision-making, has been strongly refuted in the literature (Mintzberg, 1994). Quoting Mintzberg, Khatri and Ng, persuasively argued that strategic planning is an oxymoron since planning requires analytical thinking and strategy requires synthetization of information. Khatri and Ng concluded that that is the reason why this planning approach has been unsuccessful. This view is further corroborated by Khatri and Ng's contention that the stress put on the rational approach is the chief cause for the obstacles the United States confronted in competing with foreign companies in the 1970's and 1980's.

Under the influence of various disciplines, the literature of leadership management is beginning to look at the phenomenon of intuition not as a paranormal occurrence, an eccentricity, or an endowment enjoyed by a limited number of professionals but rather, as a legitimate management decision-making process. Underlying this trend there are emerging perceptions that the process leaders employ vastly inconsistent said Familoni (2002). Consequently, larger groups of people are steering their attention to multiple alternative solutions. Overstretched executives, who deal with an information overload, are seeking to develop and trust their gut feelings and intuitive reactions more (McNaughton, 2003). By means of cutting through rationalizations and intellectualities, they seek to arrive at the heart of complex issues more rapidly and completely. With the increasing pace of change and mounting uncertainty, it is understandable that the alternative of looking within for answers is receiving increased attention.

Andrew Cohen (2003) contended that humanity is in a state of crisis. Aranha and Martins (2005) said this crisis originates from the collapse of reason and rationality. Only by taking the risk to leap into a higher consciousness does it stand the chance to free itself from the problems it has created. Indeed, there is a sense of emergency pervading society and the corporate arena. Such a predicament extends to leadership decision-making (McNaughton, 2003). The uncertainty and resulting perplexity is leading business leaders to more and more turn within for answers said McNaughton (2003).

There are other reasons that account for the emergent interest in intuition: First, new belief systems flooding into old cultures because of increased mobility–and exchange–between East and West, as well as globalization. Second, the influence of quantum physics discoveries on virtually all scientific fields (Zukav, 1991). Lastly, new advances in neurophysiologic research have increased interest. (Kopeikina, 2006). Furthermore, the dawn of postmodern resurgence elicited the need for a paradigm shift in leadership competencies (Familoni, 2002). The current state of turmoil the world is in is largely the result of a discontentment with the traditional objective, Comptian reductionist worldview. It is conceivable to assert that there is a revolution, and perchance an evolution, occurring in human thought. The purely empirical belief systems of premodern cultures are collapsing. Quantum physics has shown that the objective, palpable world as we know it, if reduced to its atomic structure, amounts to nothing more than pure energy.

Therefore, the concepts of space, time and even reality are subjective constructs and, as such, are highly pliable to the "vast possibilities" (Anderson, 1933, p xii) of the human psyche. From this prism, Anderson (1933) noted that the path to decision-making lies at the heart of every individual.

Parikh (1994) contended that intuition could no longer be ignored as a legitimate and compelling decision-making tool for executives confronted by the speeding up of transformations and revolutions in the business environment. Leaders who can masterfully access their intuitive skills may be at an advantage to seize fleeting prospects in a fluid environment to maximize the chances of winning in the business arena. The concept of intuition, as a conduit connecting the conscious and the subconscious (Parikh, 1994), leads to decision rapidity on the level of other brain functions. Superior leaders seem to possess this ability, quickly evaluating a situation and confidently acting upon their inner guidance (The Idea Bridge, 2002).

The Phenomenon of Intuition

The phenomenon of intuition has been part of humanity's attempt to attain the answer to life's most pressing problems for millennia. The universality of the interest on intuition reflects in the vast literature of human civilization. The religious scriptures (Covey, 1989); the writings of classical, modern and post-modern philosophers (Werner & Pluhar; 1999; Philippe, 2002; Baggini & Stangroom, 2003; Aranha & Martins, 2005; Homer & Westcott, 2005; Medina & Wood, 2005; Reale, 2005; Zingano, 2005); and mathematicians such as Descartes (Pietroski, 2002) have paid tribute to intuitive powers as a genuine tool to the achievement of knowledge.

Given its elusiveness, diametrically opposed definitions of intuition have created much debate. Philosophers, psychologists and the public harbor a variety of meanings often generating conflict and misinformation. Furthermore, throughout the literature intuition is frequently erroneously referred to interchangeably with tacit knowledge, instinct, irrational thinking and mystical abilities. Burke & Miller (1999) contended that:

> [c]ontroversies and a bad reputation of intuition are results of prevailing lack of understanding, unfounded generalizations, and varying and often conflicting interpretations in the research literature. Several constructs have been used interchangeably with intuition. However, tacit knowledge has been differentiated from intuition, and implicit learning. (p.1)

A variety of disciplines has focused on the phenomenon of intuition– from philosophy (Moser & vander Nat, 2003) to psychology and management (Jung, 1973; Patton, 2003) and the ensuing result was the creation of various conceptual definitions. Even though religious, scientific, and organizational literatures have offered various, and sometimes contrasting, perspectives on intuition, there is a deficiency of adequate epistemological and contextual definitions of intuition (Rowan, 1986; Patton, 2003). Therefore, in order to understand the concept of intuition, it is necessary to consider the etymological roots of the word. Deriving from the Latin *intueri* where *into* means at or on, and *tueri* means to perceive, "to watch over," (Online Etymology Dictionary, 2001, ¶ 1), the word intuition implies the idea of an inner experience. In fact, numerous authors often refer to intuition as the inner voice (Familoni, 2002).

From a scholastic philosophical point of view, The Oxford English Dictionary (2006) defines intuition as "the spiritual perception or immediate knowledge" (p.1); and from a modern philosophical perspective, as "the immediate apprehension of an object by the mind without the intervention of any reasoning process" (p.1). In the realm of philosophy, intuition appears as a priori knowledge stemming from the self. Intuitive knowledge opposes empirical knowledge, which relies on "sensory experience and the empirical use" (Moser & vander Nat, 2003, p. 19). Numerous philosophers offered elaborate conceptualizations of intuition as a phenomenon that, in a single act of the psyche, immediately and directly grasps the truth in its entirety without reliance on evidence of sensorial experience (Jung, 1973; Yogananda, 2003; Chaui, 2003; Moser & vander Nat, 2003; Pounds, 2006). Unlike empirical knowledge, intuition is not concerned with the details but with grasping the whole knowledge at once (Jung, 1973; Yogananda, 2003). Yogananda (2003) purported: "Neither the senses nor the power of inference that builds knowledge on sense testimony can be trusted to tell us the truth about the universe, our earth, the human body, or the mind" (p.468).

This definition is of particular importance since it hinges on post modernistic trends towards global and universal thinking. In the realm of psychology, intuition appears as the non rational function of consciousness and as an intrinsic component of emotional intelligence (Jung, 1973; Cooper & Sawaf, 1997; Goleman, 1998).

Quoting Sowerby (2001), McNaughton (2003), in a heuristic study, offered a transpersonal perspective by stating that intuition originates from a higher plane of spiritual or divine consciousness. In the study, participants described their intuitive experiences. Of particular relevance were the respondents' statements that intuition derived neither from memory, nor subconscious, nor past experience. Although these are accepted rational means of knowing, they can be sources of delusion and error (Aranha & Martins, 2005).

In the business circles, leaders refer to the term intuition as insight, hunch, or gut feeling, or even smell (Rowan, 1989; Goleman, 1998; Cooper & Sawaf, 1997). Philosophically oriented descriptions emerged with management scholars such as Covey (1989) who called intuition the inner compass. Goleman (1998) referred to it as the "inner rudder" (p.51). Garmston (2006) equates intuition to macro thinking and holistic analysis, associating it to high-performing teams. Nonetheless, executives are reluctant to admit to the use of intuition, affirmed Familoni (2002) paraphrasing Agor (1968).

Persuasive arguments clarifying the use of intuition originated from the psychological sciences. It was owing to the developments in humanistic, Gestalt, and transpersonal psychology in the 1970s that intuition became an object of scientific investigation. A preoccupation with mind expansion and listening to the inner voices characterized personal and transpersonal psychology research. Such studies were the predecessors of the emerging management and organizational literature on the subjective aspects of decision-making (Church, 2005).

According to Wren (2003), Mary Parker Follett's Gestalt orientation to an introspective and holistic approach to organization and management learning greatly influenced the thoughts of Herbert Simon (1947) a Nobel laureate. Simon and Mintzberg were the forerunners of the discussions of intuition as a component in management decision-making. Those germinal ideas were significant to the development of the theory of organizational effectiveness. A significant input in the history of intuition in management came from the Simon's his conviction that "neither human thinking and decision-making, nor human creativity need be mysterious" (Frantz, 2003, p. 1). Simon applied the same views to intuition. Regarding the general perception of intuition as a paranormal phenomenon, Frantz opined that "intuition is not a process that operates independently of analysis; rather, the two processes are essential operational components of effective decision-making systems" (¶ 33). Simon's views converge with Khatri and Ng's (2000) contention that intuition and rational thinking are necessary elements in sound decision-making.

It seems that Simon was not alone in his interest in intuition. Frantz (2003) cited Adam Smith; John Stuart Mill; Alfred Marshall; John Maynard Keynes; Joseph Schumpeter; and Frank Knight as some of the illustrious theorists who wrote about intuition. Quoting Barnard (1942), Frantz (2003) proposed that Simon's philosophical views about intuition were an offshoot of Chester Barnard's book *The Functions of the Executive*. In that study, Barnard examined intuition from various angles.

Barnard defined intuition by addressing five key intrinsic points: (a) intuition is not abstract because it emerges from the subconscious almost instantaneously, and devoid of reasoning; (b) intuition does not follow a sequential, rational process; however, it is "as much an expression of intelligence as is logic" (Frantz, 2003, ¶ 8); (c) people must explore the usefulness of intuition; (d) a great number of people resort to intuition at work but are derided; and (e) intuition is most effective when used under time pressure and lack of information. Owen (2002, p.84) put forward a similar argument: "Intuition requires no steps of reasoning: no intermediate ideas need be found". Frantz (2003) proposed similar notions by quoting Barnard's prophetic views:

> Understanding of organizations also calls for intuition. Our logical methods and our endless analysis of things have often blinded us to an appreciation of structure and organization… You cannot get organization by adding up the parts…To understand the society you live in; you must *feel* organization, which is exactly what you do with your non-logical minds. (¶ 8)

Frantz (2003) said that Herbert Simon reached a different conclusion. Simon did not agree that intuition was non-rational; but rather, a rational, albeit not conscious, analytical method of decision-making. He concluded that intuition amounts to a subconscious pattern recognition. Dane and Pratt (2004) address the same subconscious dimension of intuition even though the authors make use of the term "non conscious" (p.2). Both terms seem to be interchangeable in this context.

Following Simon (1947), Wren (2003) adopted the term 'bounded rationality' (p. 271). He believed that human beings were limited in their ability to grasp the present and anticipate the future and therefore were incapable of achieving the best possible solutions. Neurophysiologic discoveries on the different capabilities of the brain's two hemispheres support that assertion. Patton (2003) contented that there are limitations to the attention span in human being's reasoning power.

McNaughton (2003) proposed that among the earlier notable proponents of intuition who stand out are Isenberg (1984); Keegan (1984); Weston Agor (1986); and Henry Mintzberg (1994), from the McGill University of Faculty Management whose writings about intuitive thinking rank among the classical and germinal literature. Their studies brought to public awareness that intuition plays a role in the daily decision and strategic planning of executives and is not inferior to rational thinking. Quoting Maslow (1968), Korac-Kakabadse, Kakabadse, and Kouzmin (2003) stressed the detachment, the independence, the self-governing character of intuitive people, their tendency to look within for guiding values and rules to live by, and to listen to the inner voices. Weston Agor (1986) developed a questionnaire instrument that measured intuition ability–the Agor Intuition Measurement (AIM). Thousands of executives across a number of industries were administered the questionnaire. The AIM consists of a survey comprised of 12 questions. High scores on the AIM survey correlates with superior decision-making skills and the use of intuition.

Intuition from the Western Perspective

In the Western world, the genesis of the discussions on intuition can be found in the philosophical domain with the epistemological allegories of the pre-Socratic Greek philosophers–Parmenides, Heraclites–as well as Plato and Aristotle–representatives of the rational intuitive process of acquiring knowledge (Moser & vander Nat, 2003; Reale, 2005). The first incursions made on the subject of intuition originated with Plato and his followers who proposed that knowledge originated from a metaphysical plane of pure and perfect ideas that is eternal and rules all physical manifestation. The Greeks believed that human beings have an a priori apprehension of these metaphysical truths (Moser & vander Nat, 2003). Therefore, it was customary for the ancient Greeks to seek advice from the intuitive readings of the Oracle at Delphi "on matters of personal and political importance" (Schmidt, 1995, p. 16). Centuries later, medieval and modern philosophers, such as Descartes (Chaui, 2003) and Kant (Pluhar, 1999) expanded on this foundational understanding of intuition in the light of the origin of human knowledge apprehension.

Intuition is a universal theme that has enthralled thinkers of all times, all cultures and disciplines. Artists, writers, poets, physical and meta physical scientists, educators and philosophers have sought, through their work, to reach the highest form of wisdom. Gary Zukav (1990) reported that modern and postmodern thinkers, such as Anderson, psychologists, such as Maslow and Jung; and physicists such as Einstein and Bohr had a "great vision that comes from beyond the personality" (p.13). Zukav was alluding to a *multisensory* realm beyond reason and logic.

Descartes provided a philosophical argument in favor of intuition that affected the whole of modern philosophy by means of his celebrated phrase: *I think, therefore I exist* (Chaui, 2003). It was during that period that the notion of an inner truth (intuition)–divinely revealed, superior to human reason, unquestionable and irrefutable–came into consciousness. The religious connotation of this view seems to be largely responsible for the prejudice held against intuition in modern times.

Nonetheless, influenced by Aristotelian ideas, medieval philosophers held a rationalistic alternative view believing that the plane of ideas does not lie apart from the physical world. Therefore, one grasps knowledge by means of sensorial experience and the rational mind (Moser & vander Nat, 2003). Aristotelian views have deeply permeated Western thought, where *to see is to believe*, until the end of the 19th century. More recently, its tenets have provided the foundation for extensive research on critical thinking. Although not a proponent of intuition, Emmanuel Kant (1724-1804) devised a synthesis of the two currents of thought by proposing what he termed the synthetic cognition (Pluhar, 1999). Kant maintained that whatever is available to us to understand depends on intuition, which is nothing else but a form of sensibility (Moser & vander Nat, 2003). Kant's arguments intended to illustrate the limitations of human being's reasoning power. Positivism and determinism heralded the birth of modern philosophical thought whose central and single tenet was logical reason. In the XIX century, Kant settled the controversy by proposing a synthetically integrative dialogue between rational and intuitive thought. Post modernistic thinking, on the contrary, is showing an increasing infatuation with the metaphysical realms—or subtler planes of consciousness—as they are frequently defined in popular literature—thus elevating subjective experience, emotion, and intuition to the status of a valid approach to knowing (Jankowski, 2002).

Intuition from the Eastern Perspective

In the East, earlier than the birth of Greek philosophy, reflections about intuition could be found in the sacred manuscripts known as The Bhagavad-Gita— which most scholars deem to be comparable to the Tao Te Ching, the Bible, the Torah, the Koran and other accepted spiritual texts (The Bhagavad-Gita Trust, 1999, ¶ 2). These ancient texts emphasize intuition over intellectual knowledge. As Capra (1991) stated:

> Hinduism, Buddhism, and Taoism are interested in intuitive wisdom, rather than in rational knowledge. Acknowledging the relativity and limitations of the world of rational thinking, Taoism is basically, a way of liberation from this world, and is, in this respect, comparable to the ways of Yoga or Vedanta in Hinduism, or to the Eightfold path of the Buddha. In the context of Chinese culture, the Taoist liberation meant, more specifically, liberation from the strict rules of convention. (p.125)

According to the Chinese thought, the application of logic by the rational mind belongs in artificial world humankind created, along with social etiquette and moral values. From the Chinese perspective human intellect and extensive knowledge alone are not synonymous with true knowing and therefore, can never comprehend the profundities of the universe or human experience, said Capra.

Intuition is a phenomenon that, in a single act of the psyche, immediately and directly grasps the truth in its entirety without reliance on evidence of sensorial experience (Yogananda, 2003; Chauí, 2003; Moser & vander Nat, 2003). Unlike empirical knowledge, intuition is not concerned with the details but with grasping the whole knowledge (Jung, 1973; Yogananda, 2003). The holistic apprehension of reality is a theme that emerges across literatures as a goal worth achieving.

The average human being is normally conscious of the rational and analytical functions of the physical mind; exclusively. The subconscious levels "lie outside the real of the ordinary waking state; hence the terminology non-conscious states or altered states of consciousness" (Schmidt, 1995, p.37). Manifestations of these levels of awareness meet with fear, rejection, and prejudice. Lack of understanding and information are the reasons why our society does not encourage the development of these legitimate and natural gifts. However, the early Greek philosophers proposed that everyone possesses the ability to perceive beyond the physical senses. Although a case for social repression may be a possible conception, it is closer to the truth to say that these powers of the mind are dormant. The result is that because these abilities possess a finer, more subtle, and quicker vibratory rate, they also require a finer, and higher vibration, affirmed Schmidt. Therefore, as long as the individual does not stimulate these mental capacities and raise his or her vibratory level, the deeper recesses of the psyche remain "preconscious, inaccessible to awareness except through serendipitous events which trigger intuitive insight into manifestation (p.39).

Towards a Postmodern Definition of Intuition

A central notion to postmodernist philosophy is the idea of relativity in the way human beings perceive reality. The concept of absolute and certain underwent reexamination, giving way to deeper questioning regarding the validity of many a scientific theory. Thomas S. Kuhn, a representative of the post modernist movement, made the assertion that much of what scientific textbooks proclaim is a combination of misleading ideas that result from competing paradigms that invalidate one another over time (Larry Ross, Lecture in course PHL 717, in April 2004). Once a paradigm is unable to solve a problem, it falls in disuse thus affecting the way society functions.

Changing paradigms provoke successive scientific revolutions but none of them is capable of resolving the conflict among the competing theories. The problem is that none of the pre-modern and modern theories explained phenomena in their entirety. Ross remarked that no two scientists are able to perceive a phenomenon in the same manner. Addis & Podestà (2005) echoed Ross's views in that one of the foremost concepts of postmodernism the criticism of the modern empirical outlook on the world as an objective reality is actually a mix of constructs of millions of individuals bound together by different contexts. Therefore, by acting and using both their rationality and intuition individuals can de facto contribute to create change the professed reality, but above all, change the way they perceive it.

The shift in the way the world sees and conceives reality appear to point to be steering toward the increased need to replace rational modes, said Ross.. Towards this post modernist goal, thinkers are reaching back to antiquity, to reformulate and inquire about many of the accepted axioms (Ross). Evidence of this trend comes forward in the works of management theorists who exhibit ideas expounded in the pre-Socratics, and in the works of Eastern masters.

Stephen Covey (1989) affirmed that there are essential, innate universal truths that the individual can access. This view converged with Yogananda's (2003) assertion that intuition transcends duality and reaches maximum truth at any given time. Cooper and Sawaf (1997), quoting Einstein and Emerson, affirmed that intuition is what really matters since it is the highest wisdom. Cooper and Sawaf placed intuition on the zenith of a growth continuum–what they term "the fourth cornerstone" (p. i). Cooper & Sawaf recognized that the voice of intuition speaks through emotions, in "a place where mind could no longer produce the type of data that they wanted" (p.12) beyond time, space and matter.

Intuition, Quantum Physics, and Leadership

Theoretical physics and the business arena seem to share similar principles besides mathematical equations applied to finance: both deal with uncertainty and chaos; both live in a "quantum age...and invisible fields that shape behavior" (Wheatley, 1999, p. vii); both gravitate in a world of interrelationships, and interconnections. Arntz, Chasse, and Vicente (2005) affirmed that: "[q]uantum physics is probabilistic: You can never know with absolute certainty how a specific thing will turn out (p. 55)." Arntz, Chasse, and Vicente further explained that:

> Classical physics is reductionist: It was based on the premise that only by knowing separate parts could you eventually understand the whole. Perhaps more importantly, quantum physics has erased the sharp Cartesian distinction between subject and object, observer and observed that has dominated science for 400 years." (p.56)

Thus, quantum theory challenges beliefs about objective measurement, and deterministic prediction (Zukav, 1990; Wheatley, 1999). Although expressed differently, this notion converges with Capra's (1991) ideas about the study of subatomic physics. Capra stated that "the constituents of matter and the basic phenomena involving them are all interconnected, interrelated and interdependent; that they cannot be understood as isolated entities but only as integrated parts of the whole" (p.131).

In the context of organizational leadership, quantum postulations bespeak of "new possibilities for how to create order" (Wheatley, 1999, p. 57) in which organizations would be an interconnected web and instead of analyzing and predicting, individuals would be "acutely aware of what is happening now" (p.38). In a similar way, Parikh (1994) contended that intuition relates to the way leaders manage the current state of things. Seeming to echo Einstein's words that intuition is everything (Zukav, 1990), Capra (1991) also extolled the value of intuition to scientific creative breakthroughs. Schmidt (1995) observed that much of the recent discoveries and increased understanding of subatomic physics are recurring themes expounded by the Vedic traditions whose principal tenet is manifested reality is an illusion. This juncture of science and spirituality marks a confluence between Eastern and Western thought, which may lead to the needed "evolution of human consciousness of which intuition plays a quintessential role" (Schmidt, 1995, p. 37).

Intuition and Brain Research

The scientific and management fields received the impact, in the recent decade, of the discoveries of how the brain functions. In the 1950's, discoveries of neurophysiologic research about the role played by the corpus callosum in connecting the brain's two hemispheres represent the hallmark of scientific understanding of the brain functions as a foundation of decision-making process (Bass 1990; Patton, 2003). The brain's left hemisphere is responsible for the linguistic and mathematical abilities whereas the brain's right hemisphere oversees the artistic, holistic and intuitive aspects. Despite arguments to the contrary, "intuition continues to object to mind-brain identity" (Papineau, 2002, p.161).

Knowledge about how information is processed, received, stored in memory, interpreted and retrieved at later stages has changed child and adult education, leadership, organizational behavior, and strategic management (Goleman, 1996; Perkel, 2004). The breakthroughs in understanding of the mechanisms of the right-brain hemisphere in particular –where intuition and synthesis predominate–have contributed to an appreciation of management and leadership styles. Hayes, Allinson, and Armstrong (2004) argued that conventional management tactics would be greatly enhanced if "supplemented by right brain skills because making sense of the complexity that confronts managers requires holistic, lateral, intuitive thinking" (p.3).

It is widely accepted now that high levels of information processing occur in the right brain hemisphere. Kumar and Dempsey (2002) posited that there is a relationship between the right hemisphere dominance and intuitive functions and emotions. The right hemisphere is found to be responsible for planning, visualizing, and exercising good judgment (Perkel, 2004). Neurophysiologists McCraty, Atkinson and Bradley (2004) studied intuition as "a process by which information normally outside the range of conscious awareness is perceived by the body's psycho physiological systems" (p.1). Regarding the participation of the brain in intuitive thinking, McCraty, Atkinson and Bradley affirmed that intuition is a "system-wide process in which both the heart and the brain (and possibly other bodily systems) play a critical role" (p.1) and demonstrated, by a holographic principle, how "intuitive perceptions accesses a field of energy into which information about 'future' events is spectrally enfolded" (p.1).

Thousands of years ago, quoting Hippocrates (460-377 B.C.), Reimer (2004) had already stipulated that the brain is the sole domain of the emotions. These assertions seem to establish a relationship between the emotions and intuition. In the field of management, Goleman (1996) and Perkel (2004) perceived a clear relationship between the emotional intelligence and its competencies–intuition being one of them–and business success.

Psychologists have described intuition as the non rational function of consciousness and as an intrinsic component of emotional intelligence (Jung, 1973; Goleman, 1998; Cooper & Sawaf, 1997). Alexander Pope (2005) brought new light into the discussion by saying that theorists confuse intuition with instinct. The latter is purely physiological. Therefore, intuition differs from instinct, conditioned reflex or any other physiological activity. Instinct and other subliminal biological operations are physical. Intuition is an intellectual activity since much epistemological, logical and other elemental thinking occurs underneath conscious awareness. This difference is crucial to the understanding of intuition.

In his breakthrough book *Emotional Intelligence,* Daniel Goleman (1996) suggested that human beings possess two minds, a rational mind and an emotional mind "which affect work-related interactions and behaviors" (Brown, 2003, p.3). Emotions are built-in response mechanisms to external stimuli whose purpose is to decode outer events, translate them into an internal, subjective language in order to prompt human beings to make decisions (Brown, 2003). This mechanism is essential for effective survival and decision-making. If deprived of this basic life system component, individuals are incapable of functioning. Brown (2003) mentioned that research has investigated the important role emotions play in intuitive decision-making. Brown said that:

> Persons with brain damage to neocortex and limbic system linkages reported to have an extremely hard time making good decisions or even making decisions at all. Deprived of the intuitive signals that guide most of us in decision situations–what Damasio calls "somatic markers" or gut feelings related to experience–these people depend entirely on a computer-like logic process that does not assign emotional values to different possibilities. Thus deprived, or emotionally unaware, they struggle with everyday decisions; they are easily stymied and prone to making consistently poor choices, as suggested by a card-selecting experiment. (p. 1)

Intuition and Spirituality in Organizational Leadership

The increasing focus of management literature in spirituality in the workplace is leading researchers to establish a connection between intuition and spirituality, and leadership performance and efficiency in organizations. (2001), in their study about executives' perceptions of spirituality, urge organizations to increase their commitment to spirituality. Ashar & Lane-Maher (2004) found a positive correlation between being successful and spirituality. Marques (2005) defined this trend as:

> An experience of interconnectedness and trust among those involved in a work process, engendered by individual goodwill; leading to the collective creation of a motivational organizational culture, epitomized by reciprocity and solidarity; and resulting in enhanced overall performance, which is ultimately translated in lasting organizationalexcellence. (¶ 18)

Underlying this trend there are a growing perception and conviction that today's corporate world needs to undergo a dramatic transformation concerning its procedures and cultures. Several authors are of the opinion that spirituality does not have neither a religious connotation nor implication and define spirituality as the core practice, value and awareness of innovative, friendlier and effective organizations. By incorporating values such as human creativity, empowerment, fostering self-leadership, and ethical behavior into their human resources and business strategies, organizations can achieve higher measures of health, happiness, wisdom, self-development, success, and fulfillment through service to others. Accomplishing that degree of realization can lead to increased intuition that in turn can lead to enhanced creativity and expansion (Lips-Wiersma, 2002; Heaton, Schmidt-Wilk, & Travis, 2004; and Marques, 2005).

Intuition in the Business Environment

In the organizational environment, intuition has traditionally been associated with the feminine gender (Tischler, Biberman, and McKeage, 2002). Nonetheless, intuition is acquiring the status of a legitimate tool leaders utilize in the decision-making process (Khatri & Ng, 2000). Cooper and Sawaf (1997) stated intuition supports work and leads to creativity. Further, practical intuition is an integral facet of emotional intelligence and correlates positively with the successful performance of organizational leaders (Koretz, 2000).

Tuttle's (1988) findings about intuition regard it as being educable and to have significant implications for virtually all educational situations, particularly in such areas as creativity, cooperativeness, and altruism. Stephen Porth (2003) in an introductory investigation about the increasing interest and concern with spirituality in all facets of business life purported this is a subject that ranks high on the list of organizational concerns. The author found that religiousness, faith, intuition and ethics as manifestations of spirituality had a direct impact on leadership, teamwork, conflict resolution and decision-making.

Fisher (1999) observed that modern leaders today are overstretched, having to contend with ambiguity and uncertainty resulting from accelerated change and the information overload. Vaill (1996) speaks to leaders in the community about working productively in "turbulent environments… where the 'firm' is not so firm anymore" (p. xi). Cohen (2003) described humanity's current state of being as a desperate crisis. On all spheres of life, awareness that a significant change must occur is weighing on perplexity and fear.

Fisher (1999) concludes that real leaders will need to develop intuition, and the wisdom that comes with it, if they want to be capable of leading and making the right business choices for their organization and their employees. Arntz, Chasse, and Vicente (2005) observed that human beings sole belief on what they can see with their physical eyes has been so ingrained in the human thinking mode for so long, even though modern quantum physics have demonstrated, experimentally, that much of what man perceives as concrete may not be real from a sensory perspective.

Intuition and the Organizations of the Future

Futurists are unanimous in predicting that the human reasoning abilities to apprehend the overwhelming avalanche of diverse and wide-ranging information will decrease as the pace of change increases and the world becomes more complex (Schmidt,1995). The awakening of the intuitive capacity is the solution for worldwide transformation, affirmed Schmidt. Our mechanistic, detail-oriented models of thinking become *passé* in moments of leadership. They belong in the reactive mode and are reserved for those who prepare to execute the vision and the strategic plans (Khatri, Ng, & Lee, 2001).

Even with all the pieces in place, the stunning speed of events, their consequent changes, the instability and turmoil they cause, will still pose threats and challenges to world's leaders in any sphere, in any microcosms. Organizations seem to be well equipped with detail and technique-oriented managers and leaders. Logical, systematic thinking can and ought to combine with intuition for enhanced performance (Kutschera, 2002). Parikh (1994) pointed that Charles M. Schwab (1862-1939), the American steel magnate and first president of the US Steel Corporation, seemed to be keenly aware of the fact that success in business depends on imagination and a vision of the situation as a whole.

The reductionist approach seems to lean toward breaking apart our understandings and conceptual approaches, and it is rampant. Even though the more contemporary systems approach attempts to integrate different organizational components, it still separates things into discrete parts and boxes such as in a flow diagram thus compartmentalizing and creating conflict. The disasters sweeping the globe at present are likely to happen again in the future, thus confronting leaders and organizations with the need to be looking for ways to bring things together (Wheatley, 1999).

Intuition and Decision-making

Scholars have argued that decision-making is central and intrinsic to leadership (Simon, 1959; Korda & Lynch, 1990; Bass, 1990; Vaill, 1996; Andersen, 2000; Krishnan, 2001; *Tischler, Biberman, & McKeage*, 2002; Linder, 2003; Kazlev, 2004; Starratt, 2005; Symonds, 2005; Jentz & Murphy, 2005; Miller & Ireland, 2005; Rorrer & Skrla, 2005). Despite the plethora of valuable decision-making models currently existing in management literature, most of them are incomplete (Andersen, 2000). Andersen (2000) contributed to the understanding of management decision-making in organizations by presenting an eight-fold decision-making model based on an application of Jung's classical four functions: (a) intuition; (b); feeling; (c) thinking; and (d) sensation. The adapted decision-making model comprises: (1) intuition with thinking (as auxiliary function); (2) intuition with feeling; (3) thinking with intuition; (4) thinking with sensing; (5) sensing with thinking; (6) sensing with feeling; (7) feeling with sensing; and (8) sensing with intuition. In the decision-making process, one function will always be dominant; one auxiliary; one underdeveloped; and one unconscious (Andersen, 2000). According to Carl Jung's psychological theory of types, decision-making process stems from a combination of four functions of consciousness. Such functions–or abilities–are interdependent ways humans use to perceive reality (Kazlev, 2004). Quoting Keegan, (1984) Andersen (2000) contended that:

> The typology theory of Jung is almost complete in the sense that it touches on both functions of perception and both functions of judgment and their relationship to each other… and has withstood the test of time in the fields of psychology and Psychiatry. In the field of management development, the typology presented by Jung gives a genuine insight into the question why personssucceed or fail in their decision-making, and how they do it. (p. 2)

It is important to note that, in the psychological typology offered by Jung, intuition and sensing designate perception functions, says Andersen (2000). However, according to Bass (1990), it was Barnard the first to draw attention to the rational and intuitive components of successful executive decision-making. These original ideas still prevail today. Bass posited that Simon later expanded upon Barnard's theory by differentiating unconscious intuitive decision-making from conscious rational decision-making. Nonetheless, the notion that analytical thinking is conducive to more effective decisions still prevails in the preferred decision styles of leaders as well as research on decision-making (Khatri & Ng, 2000; Blotnicky, 2002).

Evidence in the literature presents three factors as possible causes for this phenomenon. First, the remnants of the European rationalistic approach to problem solving are still prevalent in the modern educational system (Freyre, 1973). Second, the tendency of management to overemphasize current technology and "to adapt to existing circumstances while failing to maintain a reasonable amount of flexibility for the future" (Miller & Ireland, 2005, p. 22). Third, intuition is still shrouded by prejudice (Khatri & Ng, 2000). On the other hand, empirical evidence in support of intuitive decision-making is increasing.

In a laboratory study, McMackin & Slovic (2000) found that "thinking about reasons for decisions before deciding may degrade decision quality" (p.1). The study investigated whether the characteristics of a task significantly influenced the reasoning process, affecting the quality of decisions. Specifically, McMackin and Slovic found that linear and overt reasoning tarnished judgment quality, on an 'intuitive' task. Conversely, the authors also found that "explicit reasoning enhanced performance on an 'analytic' task" (p.1). A parallel view had already been found in Eisenhardt's (1989) study about strategic decision in high-velocity environments whose findings indicated that the dichotomy between rational and non rational decision-making is limited and limiting; human beings have the capability of adopting multiple decision-making tactics when problem solving. The Multi-Criteria decision-making method advocated by Gomes, Gomes, and Almeida (2002) strongly corroborates this view. In the Multi-Criteria method, the human, subjective, and psychological factor play an undeniable and important role in the decision-making process. Such studies are contributing to an increased understanding about intuition in leadership decision-making.

Current Findings

The world's current state of crisis requires "extraordinary minds" (Mitroff, 2004, p.1). Traditional thinking approaches no longer withstand on scientific and philosophical fronts. It behooves leaders to widen these assumptions and develop new suppositions that prepare individuals and organizations for the future, maintained Mitroff. The intellectual fundamentals and premises "upon which all of our organizations and institutions are based, have crumbled" (p.1). Andrew Cohen (2003) advocated that humanity as a whole is in need of a real evolution of consciousness.

For centuries, a fragmented vision of the world has influenced science and education. One of the major assumptions has stated that, "in order for something to be or to count as a problem, it had to be stated (defined) unambiguously and precisely" (Mitroff, 2004, p.1). "[C]omplex problems do not have a single formulation" (p.1). As a consequence, "one needs to learn how to formulate problems from multiple perspectives" (p.2). Such state of affairs is ironic because, despite the fact that the world is increasingly becoming an interdependent global network with mounting complexities leaders still favor approaching problems from a fragmented perspective (Khatri & Ng, 2000). The problem is that these approaches have failed to provide fast and comprehensive solutions to new global challenges. Globalization poses problems that require a more inclusive, encompassing and wide-ranging perspective. "[I]f complex problems only exist as 'wholes', then the knowledge that is required for formulating and solving problems must be holistic as well" (p.2).

The development of sophisticated analytical management tools has made a valid positive impact on organizational management. The nature of these procedures entails investment risk analysis, multiple regressions, statistical methodologies, and strategic planning (Parikh, 1994). Used as problem solving techniques, such tools were timely and necessary in the past decades. In the last decade however, managers became increasingly aware that the Cartesian approach to problem solving and decision-making did not take into account the full breadth and complexity of the postmodern world.

Confronted by new market and environmental pressures, demands and anxiety, overstretched executives deal with information overload, change rate and dwindling resources. New management tools that portray information in a simple, condensed, and linear manner have become necessary. Furthermore, the new tools need to enable executives to arrive at the heart of complex issues more rapidly and completely. The reasons behind this relate primarily to the cost associated with time losses in detecting and correcting errors that lead to performance gaps (Fulmer, 1994).

Khatri and Ng (2000) indicated that, in turbulent and fast-paced environments, intuition enables leaders to quickly evaluate a situation, integrate and synthesize large amounts of data, and decide in spite of incomplete information. Additionally, intuition has a strong positive effect on business profits, developing higher ethical conduct and standards (McNaughton, 2003), and is positively correlated with responsible risk-taking (Campbell, 2000). Further, the use of intuition, as *the hidden intelligence,* (Familoni, 2002) in strategic decision-making is a component of critical thinking (Cottringer, 2004). The benefit of such a study refers to the existing hiatus in scholarly work that explores the human natural ability to possess and develop intuitional capacities and is evident in the relevant literature.

A review of literature revealed that there is no research available comparing the decision-making process of American and Brazilian executives. Furthermore, there is no research investigating the decision-making style of bankers. A study comparing the decision-making styles of the two cultures and their perception of the role of intuition in decision-making would be not only unprecedented but of significance to the decision-making approaches of future generations of leaders and executives in Brazil and in the United States.

One of the major challenges facing bank leaders' decision-making refers to relying on scanty or temporary information, in "turbulent environments... where the 'firm' is not so firm anymore" (Vaill, 1996, p. xi). "The economic forecasts banks rely on when making business and investment decisions may not be as reliable as some bankers believe" (Linder, 2003, p. 1). Commercial banking managers, also, are not as focused on losses as they are on the uncontrollability of risk-related factors and on the probabilities associated with various undesirable outcomes. The primary concern appears to be the ability to exert some level of control over outcomes (i.e. adjust the level of risk) through the application of known standards and criteria to the decision situation. To the extent that relevant information is ambiguous or unavailable, or there are factors to which such criteria do not apply, the degree of uncontrollability increases. Nevertheless, where avenues for control are available, these are pertinent, particularly as indicated by probability assessments of negative outcomes in various areas (Pablo, 1999).

Intuition is a non-rational form of thinking and most business leaders typically view themselves as very rational (Fisher, 2000). Familoni (2002) and McNaughton (2003) stated that rational thought, as a process of interpreting information, has lost its reliability. Additionally, the accelerated pace of change, along with the resulting increase in information requires a new set of innovative set of skills. Ben S. Bernanke (2005), governor of the U.S. Federal Reserve Board, in a speech delivered to National Economists Club in Washington, D.C. on December 2, 2004, discussed how monetary policy decisions made based on limitations in information could be gravely misleading.

The behaviors supporting intuition skills were defined as the ability to think intuitively, and to anticipate future trends and subtle market currents; being able to see beyond the obvious appearances, considering many simultaneous alternatives; and accepting the risk of being derided when taking a leap of faith without sufficient information. As a new leadership competency, intuition is increasingly playing a role in the decision-making process of leaders.

Khatri and Ng (2000) recommended that intuition be liberally used in unstable environments. Several factors affect effective decision-making, namely emotion, technology, team dynamics, and pace of environment (Eisenhardt, 1989; Bass, 1990; Leidner & Elam, 1994). With so many variables to contend with, leaders need an innovative decision-making skill that allows them to deal with complexity, ambiguity, in the face of uncertainties (Bass, 1990). One year later, Khatri and Ng (2000) put forward an argument based on the premise that by combining intuition and reason, organizations are better equipped to respond "in an evolutionary sound way to our problems" (p.1).

In an international survey, Korn Ferry International (2001) – one of the world's leading executive search company– revealed that the key qualities of the leader of the third millennium stand upon intuitive abilities. The qualities include: (a) Visionary – thinks intuitively, and who can anticipate future trends and subtle market currents; (b) Perceptive– able to see beyond the obvious appearances, considering many simultaneous alternatives; (c) Introspective – does not block internal stimuli; (d) Impressionable – open, and trusting; (e) Decisive – accepts the risk of being derided when taking a leap of faith without sufficient information. These descriptive characteristics depict the profile of the intuitive leader.

Michaud (2002) found that intuition is "related to effective strategic decisions" (p.3), converging with Hayashi's (2001) findings that leaders and executives often rely on intuition when making decisions. They also possess a self-checking mechanism against faulty intuition and error in judgment.

Decision-making appears to be even more challenging in the banking industry's current alarming situation. Huges, Lang, Mester, Loong, and Pagano (2002) reached a similar conclusion and noted "Bank consolidation is a global phenomenon that may enhance stakeholders' value if managers do not sacrifice value to build empires" (p. 1). Schurmans and Mavaddat (2004) reported that:

> mergers, acquisitions and bank conversions are experiencing a dramatic rise… and the consolidation of the industry will continue to take place at an accelerated pace appears to be a trend…As in the case of other industries, consolidation through mergers is fraught with challenges and myriad unexpected consequences. (p.1)

The situation is now further aggravated by the need for organizations to respond to rapidly changing markets, if they are to survive (Dane & Pratt, 2004). However, quick decisions pose a danger to the quality of decisions. Therefore, the challenge lies in achieving high-quality decisions in the lowest possible amount of time, Dane and Pratt stated. In corroboration to that statement, Rappaport (2006) maintained that at times of scarcity of "value-creating opportunities to invest in the business, companies should avoid using excess cash to make investments look good on the surface but might end up destroying value" (p.1).

Chapter Conclusion

The management literature appears to agree with the notion that intuition, as a leadership skill, is relevant and even desirable to strategic thinking. Roy Rowan (1986) when interviewing dozens of CEOS of leading American companies, observed that although the term hunch invites contempt and prejudice, it still occupies a "sacred" height about which very little transpires. Despite this secrecy, the intuitive ability constitutes a vital instrument to business leaders who place logic and analysis in the category of reinforcing accessory to a decision based on an insight or inspiration. According to Rowan, often times, business leaders admit, the final determining maneuver to victory demands a courageous intuitive leap into the unknown and the inclination to follow inner directions. Parikh (1994) stressed that the subject of intuition is rapidly becoming a key element in the business paradigm shift. Contemporary scholars adopted the notion that the journey of leadership is primarily an internal plight to connect with a higher influence (Wheatley, 1999; Sanders, Hopkins, & Geroy, 2003). Stephen Porth (2003), in an introductory investigation about the increasing interest and concern with spirituality and ethics in all facets of business life, demonstrated that intuition is a subject that is ranking high on the list of concerns in the work environment. On the other hand, the review of literature revealed four issues that seem to hamper a fuller understanding of intuition in leadership decision-making. First, the multiplicity of definitions of intuition lacks a consistent use of the term. Second, the vestiges of the cognition (logic) – emotion (intuition) dichotomy of the "dualistic philosophies of the ancient Greeks" (Jankowski, 2002, p. 2) still pervades the Western emphasis on positivistic thought. Third, there is a dualism regarding intuition as a process and an outcome (Dane & Pratt, 2004). Finally, the accepted notion that intuition is synonymous with the ability to retrieve material stored in the memory. Postmodern philosophers and theorists however, point to a mounting trend towards accepting the non-rational, emotional, and spiritual aspects of human thought, thus validating intuition as a component of decision-making.

Chapter Summary

This chapter examined intuition from philosophical, scientific, and managerial points of view. Specifically, it focused on intuition as decision-making tool in the organizational context (Khatri & Ng, 2000). Although many definitions abound, there seems to be some discrepancy among them. The underlying reason is misinformation and prejudice (Khatri & Ng). Nonetheless, all definitions seem to have a single thread connecting them: Intuition precludes the procedural, sequential, deductive steps of logical and rational thinking to apprehend truth (Jung, 1937). As Schmidt (1995) stated, from all the information that was gathered in the process of literature review, the main recurring theme pointed in the direction of a transformation that is needed to effectively deal with the challenges of an increasingly chaotic world. The "hidden intelligence" (Familoni, 2002) that emerges from the inner consciousness in the form of intuition could be the answer. However, this statement is far from being generalized. Further research is necessary among different populations and industries. A proposed scientific approach that investigates American and Brazilian bankers' perceptions on intuitive decision-making will be presented in chapter three.

CHAPTER 3: METHODS

The problem that guided this research study was that the use of the traditional analytical processes creates obstacles to the use of intuition in decision-making in banks' profitability (Dane & Pratt, 2004). To investigate the phenomenon of intuition in the context of decision-making in the banking industry among 36 American and Brazilian bank leaders, a qualitative method and a *multi-iteration* Delphi design was used to gather data. *The purpose of this multi-iterative Delphi research study was to describe and conceptualize the phenomenon of intuition in the decision-making process among 36 American and Brazilian bankers around the world,* utilizing convenience sampling and snowball sampling strategies. *The intent of this* research was to gather information about intuition from a panel of geographically dispersed bank experts and to ascertain the evolving patterns, responses, and/or explanations until consensus was possible. The presentation of the research methods was organized by eight topics: (a) the research method appropriateness, (b) research design appropriateness, (c) sample population, (d) sampling techniques, (e) data collection procedures and rationale,(f) validity of the Delphi method, (h) reliability, (i) data analysis, and (j) summary.

Ensuing approval from the University of Phoenix Internal Review Board, three bank chief executives were identified as potential panelists, and consequently, invited, via telephone and email, to participate in the study. Upon acceptance, a request was made for referrals for other potential panelists thus obeying to the prerequisites of convenience and snowball sampling strategies.

Research Method Appropriateness

The following discussion presented the appropriateness of the proposed qualitative research method, the *multi-iterative Delphi research design, and the rationale for choosing the research method and design to accomplish the intent of the study.* Creswell (2002) noted two research methods that drive research: (a) quantitative, and (b) qualitative. Quantitative research methods require a specific approach to sampling and statistical analysis (Gall et al., 2003). The quantitative methods address various questions and hypotheses that explore interventions. Quantitative designs such as descriptive, causal-comparative and correlation designs are used to study the situation *as it is.* "There are various types of quantitative studies that fall under the heading of descriptive quantitative research. This type of research "involves either identifying the characteristics of an observed phenomenon or exploring possible correlations among two or more phenomena" (Leedy & Ormrod, 2001, p. 91).

Creswell (2002) also maintained that qualitative research is an "inquiry useful for exploring and understanding a central phenomenon" (p. 648). The qualitative research method collects textual data and may include the following possible research designs: (a) case study, (b) ethnographic research, (c) phenomenological research, (d) grounded theory research, and (e) Delphi method (Adler & Ziglio, 1996). The intention of a qualitative approach is to understand the meaning of a phenomenon (Creswell). Qualitative research is grounded in the assumption that individuals construct features of the social environment as interpretations (Gall et al, 2001). Based on the core principles of a qualitative research method, the intent of this research was to use the qualitative paradigm to guide the application of the Delphi method in the investigation of the phenomenon of intuition.

Research Design Appropriateness

A discussion about the appropriateness of research design necessitates a preliminary examination of the study's intent and methodology. The intent of this qualitative research study using a Delphi design was to *describe and conceptualize the phenomenon of intuition in the decision-making process* among bank leaders on the topic of intuition. Given that the Delphi method is a multiple iteration survey technique that enables anonymous, systematic refinement of expert opinions justifies its appropriateness to this study (Helmer, 1967). The term Delphi appears in the research literature interchangeably as a technique, a process, a method, an exercise, and a survey. This research study referred to the Delphi design as a method, therefore, the Delphi method.

The objective of the Delphi method was to ensure the most dependable accord within a panel of assembled selected bank experts. In this respect, the computerized Delphi method was designed to facilitate the broader knowledge and cognitive stimulation of group thinking while minimizing disturbance. Expertise is the desired goal for panel selection, and it is this feature, that sets Delphi apart from other general forms of survey research (Clayton, 1997; Hasson et al., 2000). Thus, the assemblage of a Delphi panel of bank experts in a web environment made possible the exploration and convergence of concepts for decision-making purposes in the panelists' own time. Adler and Ziglio (1996) indicated that the Delphi members of the panel of experts are generally nominated by their peers or designated by their credentials to ensure the highest degree of precision and reliability possible in the responses. Bank panelists were formally contacted by phone and or by electronic mail following appointment by their peers.

The Delphi method has traditionally been used as a forecasting technique by using a panel of experts in a particular substantive area to predict the future based on their specialized knowledge (Olshfski & Joseph, 1991; Hasson et al., 2000). The computerized version of the Delphi method utilized in this study sought to undertake an initial exploration and probing of bank leaders' perceptions, subjective opinions, and experiences.

During the data collection phase, the Delphi method availed a sequence of questions and a Likert-type scale survey each followed by analysis and synthesis of responses (Dalkey & Helmer, 1967; Delbecq et al., 1975; Clayton, 1997; Linstone & Turoff, 2002). The purpose of the intermingled summaries was twofold: (a) to increase the experts' knowledge on the subject; and (b) to allow the panel additional opportunities to refine, and deepen their responses. The resulting distilled data was used to formulate the Likert-type scale survey items.

The appropriateness of the Delphi method was based on the following four guidelines that define the rigor of this methodology: "(a) [to] create a stronger research design; (b) [to] present more valid an reliable findings: (c) to address and minimize threats to internal validity of instruments; and (d) [to] control for bias so that the [intuition] phenomenon can be understood in an objective way" (Jacobsen, 2005, p.12). Initially used to forecast technological changes and trends, the Delphi method has been adapted for government planning, business and industry and computerized applications (Linstone & Turoff, 2002). The three main variations of the Delphi method are: (a) conventional, (b) real-time, and (c) policy (Linstone & Turoff, 2002).

According to Linstone & Turoff (2002), a successful application of the Delphi method depends largely on five cautionary measures undertaken by : (a) objective stance, (b) summarization techniques, (c) validation, (d) precision; and (e) panel participation time. Specifically, it is important to undertake a detached and objective stance to avoid the influence of subjective perspectives on the respondent group, while ensuring the representation of as large a number of diverse perspectives as possible. Exercise summarizing and presentation techniques with group responses. Validate and explore divergence of respondents' views to ensure real consensus. Avoid underrating and miscalculating the rigorous nature of the Delphi method. Recognize respondents as experts or specialists whose participation time, outside of their normal work hours, must be properly recompensed.

Given that the intent of this study was to explore executives' perceptions and conceptualizations of intuition in decision-making, and to explore themes and constructs (Gall, et al., 2002), the Delphi method was the most appropriate design. The suitability of the Delphi method to structure group communications to deal with abstract and complex issues and concepts while providing feedback on participants' contributions to increased knowledge (Linstone & Turoff, 2002) rendered it appropriate for the purposes of this study. Schmidt (1995) made the statement that the Delphi method is suitable for "identifying problems, defining needs, establishing priorities, identifying and evaluating solutions" (p.139). Schmidt emphasized that:

> The [Delphi] process includes (a) individual contribution of knowledge and ideas; (b) assessment of a subjective group judgment or view; (c) opportunities for panelists to revise their views; (d) a chance to react to view points from experts with diverse backgrounds; and (e) an opportunity to express radical and widely divergent views in a non-threatening context. (p. 139)

The computerized Delphi method was used as the research design. With the widespread use of computers for research purposes, and due to the numerous logistics, costs, and time-related advantages and benefits associated with web-based data collection, this option seemed to be the most appropriate. The number and geographic dispersion of the participants further contributed to justify the choice of the computer for open-ended questions and survey.

Traditionally, the Delphi technique has been paper based, which requires participants to be skilled in written communications. Increasingly, however, the use of electronic communications became popular requiring participants to be computer literate (Hasson et al., 2000; Linstone & Turoff, 2002). There were several advantages to the computer Delphi. Firstly, cost was reduced because experts did not have to be transported. Secondly, the computer Delphi allowed panelists to expose their opinions while preserving their anonymity. Thirdly, there was greater flexibility, as a larger number of panelists could be easily accommodated (Hartman & Baldwin, 1995). Finally, the asynchronous nature of the computer-based Delphi allowed panelists to access the website and post their responses in their own time.

The computer-based version of the Delphi method utilized in this study was configured – via a survey website – to compile and organize the panelists' data as opposed to the older version, which utilized paper and pencil – normally referred to as *conventional Delphi* (Lindstone & Turoff, 2002). According to Lindstone and Turoff, this contemporary approach is commonly termed "Delphi conference...or ...real-lucre Delphi" (p.7) because– among other advantages–its real-time communication feature is timesaving.

In sum, three features characterize the Delphi method and distinguish it from other group interaction methods: (a) anonymous group interaction and responses, (b) multiple iterations of group responses with interspersed feedback, and (c) the presentation of statistical analysis (Olshfski & Joseph, 1991; Williams & Webb, 1994; Ratcliffe, 1999; Collins et al., 2001). For these reasons, the Delphi method constituted an optimum selection for this specific research.

Population, Sampling, and Data Collection Procedures and Rationale

This section covered seven themes: (a) sample population, (b) sampling, (c) participant consent and confidentiality information, (d) data collection information, (e) data collection, (f) instruments appropriateness, and (g) instrument reliability. Although it is difficult to estimate with precision the number of bank leaders making decisions on an yearly basis, based on the size of the banks depicted on Table 1 (see chapter 1), the number of credit or financial decisions bank leaders make per year near a four-digit figure (Peter Otto Weil, July 5, 2006, informal conversation).

Sample Population

The population for this Delphi study consisted of 36 American and Brazilian senior bankers who were invited to participate as expert Delphi panelists. Thirty-five is an estimation of the number of panelists needed to reach a point of redundancy, consensus, or until no new information appears (Gall et al., 2003). The purposeful sampling of the panelists for this study was based on five criteria: (a) the nationalities of panelists; (b) the accessibility of panelists; (c) the senior ranking of the panelists' decision-making influence; (d) the diversity of job positions and bank areas allowed for higher degree of representation; and (e) the panelists had to be English speaking since the research was conducted in this language. Only panelists who met the four criteria detailed above were selected for this study.

Sampling Strategies

Careful consideration pertains to the caliber of the expert participating in a Delphi study. Ludwig (1997) affirmed that random selection is not an acceptable sampling procedure for Delphi studies. Ludwig offered three reasons: (a) random selection could hinder the group's ability to achieve its goals and objectives; (b) it does not adequately provide for appropriate selection of expertise needed to achieve the objectives of the task; and (c) the attributes and credentials of ideal respondents and a nomination process must be the prevailing rationale in selecting participants.

Given that random sampling is not a pre-requisite of the Delphi method (Schmidt, 1995), prospective panelists were selected based on non-probability methods. Galloway

(1997) proposed that non-probability methods of sampling techniques offer the following two advantages over probability sampling methods: (a) the low expenditure involved; and (b) the widely dispersed sample population in two or more different continents. With basis on these premises, a combination of convenience and snowball sampling represented adequate sampling strategies.

Purposeful sampling strategies are related to the practice of inviting panelists with rich information that is related to the purpose of the research (Patton, 2001; Gall et al., 2003). Such strategies include: (a) criterion sampling, and (b) snowball sampling, which were deemed as suitable strategies for the selection of specific panelists. Criterion sampling was used for the selection of panelists with specific criteria, as it is useful in qualitative studies to gain in-depth understanding about a group's behavior or thinking mode (Taylor & Bogdan, 1998; Patton, 2001; Orcher, 2005). The core advantage of snowball sampling was its inherent referral system that increased the population sample size (Turoff & Lindstone, 2002). Furthermore, snowball sampling was the most culturally effective in the Brazilian environment given its close banking community. Criterion sampling and snowball sampling were implemented in two steps. First, panelists were accessible through the telephone banking system and professional network. A script outlining the telephone contact introducing the study is available in Appendix G. An initial telephone contact was made, as a personal introduction, to describe the nature and purpose of the study, and to ascertain the prospective panelist's interest in the topic of intuition, and willingness to volunteer to commit time to a protracted research endeavor. Second, a written outline of the study was emailed to each potential participant along with informed consent forms (appendices A, B, C, D, and G).

Panelists who met the five criteria were contacted by telephone (appendix G) and or by electronic mail. Snowball sampling was also utilized, as it was the means used for asking well-suited panelists to recommend different well-suited panelists (Gall et al., 2003). If they demonstrated interest in the research description and were willing to participate, they were subsequently asked if they could identify other prospective panelists possessing the specified criteria. The process was repeated until the number for the population sample was achieved.

Expert panelists. Mullen (2003) disputed the selection of experts by arguing that accurate and consensual operational definitions of experts are virtually unavailable. Mullen noted the imaginary allure that surrounds alleged experts by questioning the actual benefits and caliber of responses when selecting experts as opposed to non-experts. Mullen noted that although experts are generally perceived as being "professionally or scientifically qualified and/or to have achieved high status" (¶ 25), an expert ought to be defined as any person capable of providing an input. Given that this investigation concerned the use of intuition in decision-making by bank leaders, it required experts who are representatives from the different areas of the banking industry. Therefore, selected executives with different banking expertise were invited to participate in the research study. The varying types of expertise encompassed knowledge and experience in the given area.

According to Schmidt (1995), panel sizes in Delphi studies vary widely but a "cross section of fifteen experts is sufficient for reliable results" (p.144). Conversely, Schmidt proposed the ideal panel size to be 30 participants. This view echoes Delbecq's (1975),views who maintained that 30 is an optimum number of participants, since the quality and originality of ideas tend to decline once that number is exceeded.

According to the stipulations of this study, the 36 target panelists were natives of Brazil and the United States, who either worked or resided in one of these two countries or elsewhere. Of the total 21 Brazilian panelists who participated in this study, 19 were stationed in Sao Paulo, Brazil, and two in the United States, in New York, and in Washington D.C., respectively. The first two cities are major financial centers harboring a large concentration of banks. The 11 American panelists who participated in this study came from various cities in the United States.

Research ethics.

Respect for the individual. The English language was the *lingua franca* utilized during the entire study. The Brazilian panelist contingent is fluent in English since this is the second language most commonly used in the business environment. Fluency in the English and Portuguese languages spoken in the United States and in Brazil respectively, and experience with each country's culture allowed for clear communication with the panelists. Nonetheless, in order to conform to the stipulations outlined in the Collaborative IRB Training Initiative (CITI) (2006), the option to have the consent forms translated into Portuguese was offered to the Brazilian panelists.

With regard to cultural differences between the American and Brazilian participants, even though no cultural issues were anticipated, cultural values were considered in the process of designing a research (CITI, 2006). For example, some participants might consider the topic of intuition sensitive. Since participation was voluntary, the initial telephone recruitment and briefing about the study was designed to determine those who were comfortable with the topic and therefore, would be willing and committed to participate and those who would refuse to participate. Additionally, participants were assured that they had a right to privacy and were free to decide whether to withhold response to the questions or withdraw from the study at a time of their choosing (Neuman,

1997; Creswell, 2002). A script of the telephone call (Appendix C) was submitted to IRB review before it was implemented (CITI, 2006).

The relationship among the individuals in the study was one based on trust. Considering the study was conducted by means of electronic media, when agreeing to participate, panelists were promised to have their privacy and anonymity protected and guaranteed. Even though the study was innocuous, CITI reported concerns about studies conducted via the Internet, suggesting that participants be educated about Internet security during the consent procedure. The Zoomerang survey website has a confidentiality agreement component between the host and the participant that was added on the confidentiality letter to the panelists (appendix B).

Disposal of data. Another ethics issue entailed storage, use, access and availability of research data to others (Neuman, 1997; CITI, 2006). It is tenable to affirm that the study topic was not potentially stigmatizing or prone to adversely impacting panelists' employment or reputation. However, in order to safeguard their anonymity, confidentiality measures were described in the attachment to the informed consent letter. CITI provided a few indicators to guide the design of the confidentiality letter. Firstly, panelists' identifiers were kept to a minimum as an insurance of anonymity and since they did not constitute variables in the study. Secondly, panelists' names could not be identified on the website thus anonymizing data. Thirdly, the research data was reported in aggregate form. Further, the research data was accessible exclusively by the Delphi facilitator. The data was protected from inadvertent disclosure and unauthorized access by means of passwords. The data was stored on a private file and erased from the computer to ensure and maintain confidentiality of responses. The anonymity provided in the Delphi method met the ethical requirements of this study.

Location, Informed Consent, and Confidentiality Agreements

The panelists were required to sign a form providing consent to act as a Delphi panelist before participating in the study. The consent forms were designed according to specifications by the Belmont Report (Department of Health, Education and Welfare, 1979) provided in the Appendix A. The confidentiality agreement was attached to the informed consent and the date when the form must be returned was specified. It was stipulated that if the agreement were not returned by the specified date, the potential panelist would not be invited to participate in the study. However, technical difficulties coupled with the fact that most panelists were on holiday vacation at that time, prevented the timely return of the forms. Therefore, a two-week tolerance was given. In order to ensure confidentiality and anonymity, control of the consent forms was centralized.

Data Collection Procedures

Data gathered on intuition followed the characteristics of Delphi procedures that encompass focusing on specific expert opinion on intuition by means of a successive series of rounds. Schmidt (1995) identified two forms of collecting data in a Delphi study: (a) by means of structured questionnaires extracted either from information gathered during the literature review, or (b) from the research questions.

Data collection included two rounds, the first round of a seeding nature encompassing open-ended questions, and the second round comprised of a Likert-type scale survey. Data was collected across the two rounds of the Delphi until the preponderance of responses to the points being investigated converged towards an agreement. Consensus was reached during the two rounds; the third round consisted in the presentation of results. Therefore, a fourth round was not necessary. Findings and conclusions were derived from a qualitative analysis. Based on Fowles' (1978) description of the ten steps of the Delphi method, the following list depicts the steps that were involved in this study:

1. Undertake to monitor the computerized Delphi.
2. Select the panel to participate in the study.
3. Develop the first-round open-ended questions.
4. Submit the questions to the dissertation committee's review for proper wording, in order to avoid ambiguities, vagueness.
5. Introduce the first questions to the panelists to pilot-test the questions.
6. Should questions prove appropriate, the first round responses will be analyzed.
7. Present a summary with the synthesis of the responses.
8. Based on themes that emerged from the responses to the open-ended questions, a Likert-type scale survey will be designed.
9. Analyze survey responses and present the conclusions of the study to the panelists. An illustration of the systematic process depicts the study procedural and sequential steps and the timeline (see Figure 1).

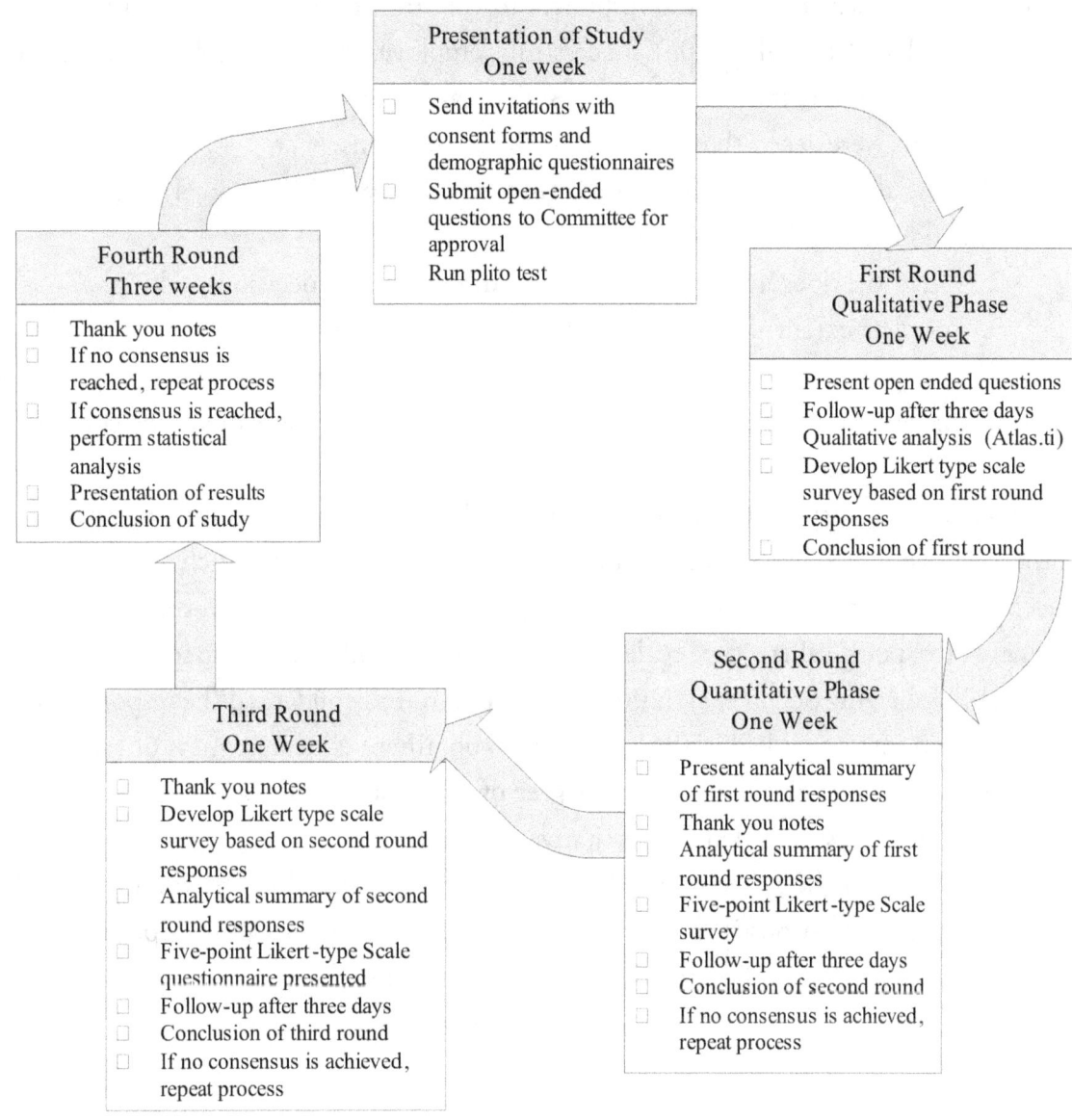

Figure 1. Delphi study procedural and sequential steps and timeline.

The purpose of the four rounds of the Delphi method was to achieve maximum input and reflection from the participants (Olshfski & Joseph, 1991; Williams, 1991; Clayton, 1997; Hasson et al., 2000; Linstone & Turoff, 2002) until responses reached a point of stability or consensus. "Ideally, iterations continue until consensus is unanimous or nearly so" (Gilsford, 1986-1998, p.4). Gilsford emphasized that in practice, perfect consensus rarely exists. Therefore, following Gilsford's prescription, the iterative process ended when panelists supported the majority of opinions.

The themes emerging from the responses to the first round were used to formulate survey items. De Vet et al. (2005) successfully employed a comparable approach in a Delphi study conducted in the educational sector, which served as a model for this study. The participants were asked the following opening questions:

1. How do you define intuition? This question was based on a similar study conducted by McNaughton (2003).
2. What role does intuition play in your daily business decision-making?
3. To what extent does intuition play a role in decision-making as it relates to strategy formulation, cost reduction and performance gaps? Some elements of this question were present in a questionnaire from an analogous study conducted by Familoni (2002).

Data collected during the first round of the Delphi was qualitative and was compiled, synthesized, codified and organized into a cohesive whole from which main themes, concepts and notions were gleaned. The emerging constructs constituted the raw material to design a five point Likert- type scale survey that was introduced on the second round of the Delphi. Following Scholl et al. (2004), the second round condensed the responses from the first round into scalable questions in order to obtain an educated guess or estimation on all topics addressed attributing some degree of importance. It is at this point that the data collection process attained a quantitative perspective.

The results from the Likert-type scale survey were compared to the results from the three open-ended questions in order to verify if there was any change of opinion in the panelists' responses or corroboration to the responses in the first round. The research map shows the sequential steps of the entire research process (see Table 3).

Table 3

Sequential Steps of the Research Process

Steps	Research Activity	Purpose
1	Submitted open-ended questions to committee members	Test for internal validity
2	Sent introduction letter confidentiality agreements and demographics questionnaires to panelists via electronic mail	Introduce study and request confirmation of participation and commitment
3	Conducted pilot test of three open-ended questions	Test for internal validity and evaluate site and quality of operational procedures

4	Sent Zoomerang Website instructions to panelists	Instruct panelists on how to access and respond to the questions
5	Launched study	Launch Round I
6	Round I of Delphi	To gain preliminary perceptions
7	Tabulated and Analyzed of Round I responses	Use responses to design survey items.
8	Present summary of results. Round II of Delphi – Likert-type scale survey	Consensus
9	Round III of Delphi – data analysis	Present summary of results.

Data Collection

Prior to the onset of the study, the panelists received an invitation letter introducing the study and its purpose, describing the research method and the anticipated time requirements for participation in the study. The purpose of the letter served as the preparatory stage and included the University registrar's office number with view to validate the student's enrollment, the Committee mentor information, and Institutional Review Board approval. Such measures were intended to increase the comfort and trust level of the participants in the study. Enclosed in the introductory letter, there was a debriefing about the location of the survey along with instructions on how to access and respond the questions to Round 1 (see appendix A) and a demographics questionnaire (see appendix B).

The data was collected through the Internet utilizing the Zoomerang survey software. Zoomerang survey software deployed the survey via the company's website ensuring anonymity and save panelists' time. Zoomerang.com, a secure Internet-based website that commercially allows organizations and educational institutions to design and dispense surveys was utilized throughout the data collection phase of the study. The three questions and the survey items for Round I and Round II of Delphi were posted on the Zoomerang website. The panelists' responses and dissemination of information were kept confidential by privately emailing a summary and feedback to each of the panelists.

The opportunity to do an asynchronous computerized Delphi utilizing the Zoomerang survey software was appropriate for this study because it centralized and facilitated the input from expert panelists. Another advantage was the immediate, accurate, and comprehensive data analysis service. Even though the Delphi method entailed successive imparting of the results during each round, the panelists remained unidentified, and therefore, anonymous to the other panelists during the study, which curtailed the possibility of group pressure and conformity.

Round I. The study pilot test was launched on December 12, 2006. The panelists were welcomed and greeted at the Zoomerang website and invited to offer comments and suggestions about the format and content of the open-ended questions. The panelists were not forthcoming in providing comments and critiques and preferred to respond to the questions.

Round I marked the beginning of the qualitative part of the study. During Round I, panelists were required to express their views freely by answering the questions from all possible angles. Information emerging from Round I was in narrative form and was analyzed outside the Zoomerang domain by utilizing the Atlas.ti software in order to identify the main themes, and constructs. The first incentive questions were broad in nature and simple in form, requesting that the panelists consider the following questions:

1. How do you define intuition?
2. What role does intuition play in your daily business decision-making?
3. To what extent does intuition play a role in decision-making as it relates to strategy formulation, cost reduction and performance gaps?

During Round I, panelists were persuaded to generate as many ideas as possible. No judgment of right or wrong applied to the answers. Therefore, panelists were free to provide examples or employ any format that would engender the relevant information required to develop the subsequent survey. The panelists were allotted one week from the time the survey was sent out, to respond to the questions. After three days, notices were sent out via telephone and electronic mail to those participants who had not responded to the questions to remind them of the deadline of Round I. At the conclusion of Round I, thank you notes were sent to each participant to encourage continued participation in the study. Additionally, a new set of instructions for the completion of Round II also accompanied the thank you notes. The thank you notes marked the conclusion of Round I, and the qualitative phase of the study. Those panelists who did not respond in the allotted time received messages thanking them for their participation. Further, such panelists were also notified of such action upon completion of Round I, and were diplomatically informed of the impossibility of further participation in the study. Subsequently, the panelists' responses were compiled verbatim, a summary of responses was anonymously circulated, and panelists were invited to reiterate or to comment on their previous responses (Mullen, 2003). The results were presented separately for each of the three questions. The former constituted the raw material to develop the Likert-type scale survey items for Round II.

Round II. Round II marked the quantitative phase of the study. In the traditional Delphi, Round II requires that expert panelists elaborate, and expand on the themes that emerged from the answers in the first round. According to the norms of the Delphi study, at this stage, the participants were given the opportunity to add comments and make amendments to the answers of the previous round. However, in a preliminary informal survey between two potential panelists, it was understood that, given the very limited time and a demanding business agenda, panelists would prefer to receive a summary only at the conclusion of the Round I instead of revisiting their responses. Therefore, even though panelists only had one chance to answer the open-ended questions, the iterative aspect of the Delphi was not lost since the panelists were still able to learn by reading the summary to Round I. From a time management perspective, this arrangement appeared to be the most applicable.

Five essential qualitative data parameters were followed in organizing the results from Round I: First, the themes or constructs that were mentioned more frequently were selected and listed separately and stood as a separate item for rating. Second, each theme or construct represented a concept or idea. Third, to minimize the risk of bias, the Zoomerang software survey tool was utilized because of it was designed to prevent tampering with the responses, which could influence the nature of the responses or the direction of the study. Fourth, given that the data from Round I was of a subjective nature, responses were evaluated for what they are worth. Fifth, the coding of the themes and constructs was succinct and jargon was avoided.

The analytical summary of Round I was forwarded to the panelists' private electronic mail addresses along with a reminder of the onset of Round II. Round II presented the set of Likert-type scale survey items requiring that panelists ranked or rated the questions according to the degree of accuracy or inaccuracy. The 5-point scale was portrayed in ascending order of consent, from *Strongly Disagree, Disagree, Agree,* to *Strongly Agree.* A neutral category–*Not Sure*–was added to allow for a broader range of views as well as to avoid leading and compelling panelists to express a fixed opinion. Each panelist was expected to check one alternative when rating each survey item to establish preliminary priorities among items. The choice of a 5-point scale seemed appropriate since, according to Birket (1986), the reliability of results is reduced beyond Likert-scale 5 or 7 categories of responses. The participants were allowed one week, from the time the survey was launched, to respond to the survey. After three days had elapsed, reminders via telephone and electronic mail address to those panelists who had not responded prompting them to be mindful of the deadline for Round II. The panelists who did not respond were notified of such action upon completion of Round II. Consequently, they were not allowed to participate further in the study.

It was in Round II where elimination of statistically negligible themes and constructs occurred. As in Round I, at the conclusion of Round II, *thank you* notes were sent to each individual panelist to show appreciation. Had not consensus be achieved in Round II, the process would have been repeated until consensual opinion was attained. Since responses to Round II reiterated the responses to Round I questions, a summary of the responses was presented to panelists in Round III thus concluding the study. As in Round I, a summary of the responses was deployed to the panelists' private electronic mail addresses. Zoomerang survey software default and automated data report presented the data analysis of responses to survey items in Round II in counts and percentages.

The data analysis availed information to the panelists about their collective perceptions and opinions. Hasson et al. (2000) supported the advantages of comparative analysis. With basis on that recommendation, the presentation of data analysis in percentages for the different perceptions of intuition enabled the panelists to have a comparative perspective.

Instrument Selection Appropriateness

In determining the appropriateness of using open-ended questions and surveys as the instruments for data collection for the target population, several factors and principles were considered, which together, formed the framework for effective data collection. The most important was to determine the existence of "information about the reliability and validity of scores from past uses of the instrument" (Creswell, 2002, p. 185). In light of the expanding scientific knowledge, Creswell cautioned against the use of instruments that may be old, obsolete, and unsuitable to the sample. Conversely, instrument development "requires knowledge about item or question construction, scale development, format, and length" (p.185). Following Creswell's counsel, parts of existing instruments from similar studies such as those conducted by Familoni (2002) and McNaughton (2003) were modified to ensure that the open-ended questions and survey items utilized were valid and reliable for the specific purpose to which they were destined. A discussion about validity and reliability of the modified instrument follows in the respective sections.

Creswell identified two types of research surveys: cross-sectional and longitudinal. "Cross-sectional surveys are employed to collect data that reflect current attitudes, opinions, or beliefs" (p.397). Since the purpose of this study was to explore the perceptions on intuition of two groups of executives, a survey design was the most appropriate instrument. Further, Creswell noted that "survey researchers collect data using two basic forms: questionnaires and interviews" (p.402). Interviews would be unfeasible given the impossibility of gathering panelists from various parts of the globe in one location for the two rounds of Delphi spanning two months.

The use of web-based open-ended questions and a Likert-type scale survey was feasible by means of the computerized Delphi capability to collect data rather quickly on a common site while respecting the panelists' personal constraints and priorities. Thus, panelists responded to the questions and survey at their own time and convenience. As a result, a greater number of ideas surfaced in the responses to the open-ended questions than in a regular survey (Linstone & Turoff, 2002). Additionally, the electronically based questions and survey included in this study were appropriate in light of the security, confidentiality and results analysis (Zoomerang, 2006).

Instrument Reliability

This Delphi study utilized the services of a survey design website titled Zoomerang. com to assist with the design and dissemination of surveys to the panelists with the objective to collect data. The sender of the survey was fully liable and accountable for managing the data collection. Nonetheless, the Zoomerang.com (2006) website bore the responsibility for site security, user access, and accurate and centralized diffusion of survey results. Market Tools, the parent company to Zoomerang.com, holds the policy of not selling, sharing, bartering, nor trading data about the research or survey respondents to the web site to external parties. Therefore, Zoomerang.com did not contact panelists for any purpose. Furthermore, the sender of the survey was solely responsible for the topics under discussion and contents of the open-ended questions and survey, whereas, the panelists were solely accountable for the themes and constructs that appeared in their response (Zoomerang. com, 2006).

Since there was a sole registered account owner, access was granted to panelists by means of an URL sent by Zoomerang. The link directed panelists to a live and active survey registered on the account determined in advance. Zoomerang.com stipulates that registration and establishment of the account with Zoomerang.com required applicable personal information, such as full name, residential address, and email address. Upon receiving this information, Zoomerang.com assigned a private account number and a site protected by a password. Further, Zoomerang.com assumed total responsibility for overall site security and protection as outlined in question 5 of the Zoomerang Online Support (Zoomerang.com, 2006, ¶ 2). "Zoomerang stores personal information of Members and Panelists in secure databases protected by passwords as well as database and network firewalls to prevent the loss, misuse or alteration of personal information". While no security systems are infallible, "Zoomerang periodically reviews and updates security measures to insure the best possible protections for member data". (¶ 1).

Security considerations. Zoomerang.com provided insurance pertaining to the panelists' electronic mail addresses. Once the panelists' electronic mail information was entered on the website's *Email List Manager*, the information was automatically sealed, and locked by the password remaining, rendering the site inaccessible to other users. The security and protection of panelists was formalized, once the *Terms of Use* were acknowledged and accepted by the sole user and account owner. In the event of breach of agreement, *Zoomerang.com* reserved the right to report unlawful conduct to the appropriate authorities, and turn over all information, including personally identifying information, to appropriate persons or entities, as well as, deactivate 's account; terminating the services (Zoomerang. com, 2006).

Validity–Internal and External

This section relates to the validity of the Delphi method, and of the instruments, that is, the open-ended questions and survey that were developed. There are two forms of validity: (a) internal validity; and (b) external validity. These types of validity were associated with the methodology–the Delphi method, and the instruments–in order to establish whether they addressed the relevant issues, so that there were no biases in portraying conclusions from the data collected and which could compromise the integrity of the data (Neuman, 1997).

Validity–Internal

Validity of the Delphi method. The validity of this study was contingent on the selection and nature of the population, that is, the expert panelists. Clayton (1997, ¶. 27) opined that "the process of selecting experts is critical to the Delphi and serves to authorize the Delphi's superiority and validity over other less painstaking and rigorous survey procedures". Neuman (1997) posited that the criteria for determining the sample size are three: (a) the level of confidence; (b) degree of tolerance to the margin of error; and (c) the degree of variability in the population under study. Neuman also mentioned a principle of accuracy, which is more frequently resorted to, that determines the sample size based on the original population domain. Larger populations permit smaller sample sizes. Neuman concluded by saying that the decision about the optimal sample size depends on three factors: "(a) the degree of accuracy required; (b) the degree of variability and diversity in the population; and (c) the number of different variables examined" (p. 222). Homogenous groups require smaller sample sizes. The fact that the population sample of this study was homogeneous in occupation but not in nationality or job function, required a higher representation from the original population domain. On the other hand, since this study did not examine variables, a sample size statistically smaller ensured the validity of the data collected, analyzed, and presented. Therefore, a balance was required. Jeffery, Ley, Bennun and McLaren (2000) suggested that an optimum size for homogenous groups is approximately 20, increasing it to prevent attrition. Bearing such factors in mind, the population for this study comprised 36 bank leaders as a representative sample.

Since responsiveness is paramount to the success of a Delphi study, it was expected that both attrition and time would potentially diminish through asynchronous Delphi rounds (Atkinson, 2001). Nonetheless, attrition did occur at a 10% rate in Round I, and 24% in Round II. Underlying reasons are discussed in chapter 4.

The Standards for Educational and Psychological Testing (1985) defined validity as "the most important implication of the centrality of the sampling process" (p.9), and "is the truism that whatever is sampled is a member of the domain from which the sample is drawn" (p.9). The Delphi method utilized in this study was subject to a strict adherence to the parameters of selection of expert panelists. Validity was assured by the "assumption of safety in numbers (i.e. several people are less likely to arrive at a wrong decision than a single individual)" (Hasson et al.2000, ¶ 29).

Regarding the indicator, the Delphi method had face validity (Neuman, 1997) in the way it explored the decision-making process of expert panelists given that it is part of the bank leaders' jobs to engage in decision-making on a daily basis. Furthermore, the Delphi method is consensus oriented which offered higher validity than decisions reached by a single individual (Brooks, 1979; Clayton, 1997; Ratcliff, 2000; Collins, 2001). Gilsford (1986-1998) posited, "in research, as in practice, consensus is rarely 100%. Practically speaking, groups have consensus at the point where they can recommend a reasonable course of action that the group will support and sustain" (p.4). In support of that, Neuman (1997) stated that the Delphi method is associated with other types of surveys that measure similar constructs; it also enjoys concurrent validity.

Validity of the open-ended questions and survey items. Another component of internal validity is content validity. Content validity is the extent to which the questions on the instrument fully embody, symbolize, represent accurately, authentically, and genuinely, and correspond to the meaning of the content (Neuman, 1997; Creswell, 2002; Salkind, 2003). Yaghmaie (2003) was of the opinion that content validity supports construct validity. This kind of validity can help to raise the level of confidence of readers and researchers about instruments employed. Content validity refers to the degree that the instrument covers the content that it is supposed to measure.

In order to establish content validity the study sought to meet two objectives: (a) the degree of each question defined the concepts of intuition addressed; (b) and the degree to which the set of questions represented the universe of dimensions and nuances (Salkind, 2003) of the concepts of intuition. The open-ended questions in Round I addressed the definition of intuition and the survey items addressed the array of nuances and aspects ingrained in the panelists' definition of intuition and its role in decision-making.

Validity

The dissertation committee and a pilot test whereby any inconsistencies emerging were eliminated before the open-ended questions in Round I were launched. As a measurement validation of the construct and its indicators, a pilot test was conducted with the participants in order to avoid "threats to internal validity" (Neuman, 1997, p. 195). The apparatus utilized in the study such as computers and survey sites and software, were also pilot tested. When the pilot test finished, every uncovered aspect of the study that needed refinement was rectified and adjusted accordingly.

The purpose of the pilot test was to elucidate concerns with the suitability of the questions. The pilot test of the questions was conducted, as an experiment in order to determine not only whether the questions fulfilled the purpose and therefore were adequate for final inclusion in the research study, but whether access to and navigation in the Zoomerang website was easier to use. There was no articulated reaction from the expert panelists to the pilot open-ended questions. Consequently, there was no need to make modifications to the open-ended questions, discontinue the instrument or have a new one developed and implemented. Round I was launched with intact open-ended questions.

The following procedural approach was developed by the San Francisco Estuary Institute (2001) and was adapted to provide equitable guidelines to oversee the pilot test process:

1. Establish the parameters and budget for the pilot test
2. Recommend specific format, approach and arguments for consideration
3. Ensure that selected format, approach and arguments conform to the study's main concerns
4. Review and comment on the initial and final questions
5. Participate in midcourse progress reviews
6. Provide feedback to the mentor and dissertation committee members about the usefulness of completed pilot test.

The raw material for the development of the quantitative instrument of this study derived from the themes and concepts emerging from the expert panelists' responses to the open-ended questions in Round I. The construct validity, "stability, consistency, and predictability" (Salkind, 2003, p.115) was established by means of a pilot test to determine whether each survey item was comprehensible and appropriate to the panelists. Thorough reviews of the expert panelists' responses were performed to ensure consistent interpretation of the data, to seek a deeper understanding and to discern for recurring themes and concepts. Any disparaging or negative information was addressed.

Survey Development Procedures

The 14 research questions (see chapter 1) comprised the framework for a cross-sectional survey (Creswell, 2002). Creswell explained that "cross-sectional designs" (p.397) are useful when comparing data that reveal opinions, concepts, beliefs, and practices from two or more different groups at one point in time. Three (qualitative) open-ended questions and one Likert-type scale survey (quantitative) comprised of 20 items were presented to the banking panelists. The final number of open-ended questions was determined after the committee's deliberation and upon receiving the approval from the committee and the IRB. Given that this was an online survey, Wright (2006) recommended the use of as few as possible questions, confirming Creswell's advice for a quick data collection. The logic was to avoid being repetitive, which might steer away from the topic, and disrespect the panelists' time. The themes emerging from the responses to the open-ended questions provided the information necessary to develop the Likert-type scale survey. The final number of items in the survey results from a combination of the aspects of intuition emerging from the open-ended questions. Therefore, attention was given to focus, applicability and concision of open-ended questions and survey items. The strategy, and criteria, for the construction of the open-ended questions as well as the survey items included "using clear language, making sure the answer options do not overlap, and posing questions that are applicable to all participants" (Creswell, 2002, p. 405). The general form for the content of the open-ended questions and survey items entailed attitudinal behavioral questions about intuition in decision-making. No sensitive and personal questions were employed.

In keeping with Creswell's (2002) recommendations and principles for question construction, the factors relating to class, gender, and cultural needs of panelists were taken into consideration. Questions and survey items were submitted to the dissertation mentor prior to the pilot test.

Pilot test. The procedures for administering the pilot test were:

1. Letter formally inviting expert panelists to participate in the study was sent
2. Expert panelists were welcomed on the website and thanked for their participation and contribution
3. Message introducing the pilot test to expert panelists explaining purpose and objectives
4. Comments, suggestions and critiques to the open-ended questions were requested
5. Delphi study launched

As stated earlier in this chapter, expert panelists were asked to volunteer to participate in the study in accordance to a systematic recruiting procedure that observed the following criteria: (a) proven nationality –from the parameters stipulated in this study; (b) profession; (c) current employment; (d) seniority; and (e) age. Creswell (2002) identified personal occurrences concerning the panelists as the most severe of threats to internal validity of a study. The only factor that might hinder the quality and reliability of this study refers to mortality, that is, panelists withdrawing from the study during the investigation process for extraneous reasons. Creswell's (2002) recommendation to tackle this drawback is to choose a larger sample to prepare for such an event. Experiment mortality is a statistical terminology Cooper and Schindler (2003) utilized to define occurrences that may change or affect in some manner the composition of the panel of experts. Although the term was primarily used in the context of experimental studies, unforeseen events such as deaths, withdrawal, attrition can threaten the internal validity of this study. In order to circumvent the probability of mortality or withdrawal during the study, as a safety margin, the total population sample was 10% larger than the required size for this study.

Validity- External

To refine the Delphi panelists' responses from the open-ended questions, a Likert-type scale survey was administered. These two rounds of data collection allowed for deeper understanding of the themes that emerged in Round I. The combined results of the qualitative and quantitative data collection underwent a validation test by means of an external audit (Creswell, 2002) where the mentor and committee members examined and commented on the different aspects of the research at the conclusion of the study. As such, credibility of the data, logical conclusions, methodological use, low statistical power researcher's bias and strategies for increasing credibility (Creswell, 2002) were addressed. Environmental factors were dealt with in the limitations section of the study.

Data Analysis

The responses to Round I were dealt with similarly as interview responses, that is, they were tabulated, compiled, and grouped into categories. Since was predicted that the qualitative data from Round I would be more detailed, in-depth, varied and extensive (Neuman, 1997), a coding system was developed. For that purpose, units of analysis for specific amounts of text were assigned a code (Neuman, 1997). This procedure was necessary, as the information content obtained from the responses to the initial round was used to design the survey items for the subsequent and final round. Furthermore, coding rules and procedures were necessary to "make replication possible and to improve reliability" (p.275).

Conceptualizations of the constructs in Round I obeyed a coding system comprised of a set of instructions and rules on how to categorize content systematically from the texts (Neuman, 1997). This coding system was tailored according to the qualitative nature of the responses. For this reason, information from the responses was categorized and classified according to three characteristics: (a) unit of analysis–in this case, units of language–which refers to words, phrases and themes; (b) frequency in which these units occurred; and (c) intensity which refers to the "strength or power of a message" (p.275).

Neuman (1997) identified two coding modalities in content (qualitative data) analysis: (a) manifest coding; and (b) latent coding. Manifest coding analyses the "visible, surface content in a text" (p.275) and can be exemplifies by the number of times a phrase, expression, or word appears in a written text. The coding system selected recorded the relevant written representations i.e. the words, constructs, phrases, themes or expressions. This process was accomplished by using the Atlas.ti computer software that searched for the specific written representations, count them and compiled them. The result was a "comprehensive list of relevant words and phrases" (p.275).

Manifest coding has high reliability because of the tangibility of the written representation. In other words, "the phrase or word either is or is not present" (Neuman, 1997, p.275). Manifest coding is confined to identifying and registering words or phrases; it does not classify nor does it analyze words or phrases. However, owing to the likelihood of a multiplicity of meanings a word or expression can connote, manifest coding can limit the measurement validity.

Latent coding–also referred to as semantic analysis (Neuman, 1997)–is concerned with the "underlying, implicit meaning in the content of a text" (p.276). Latent coding is a function of the knowledge of the language used to discuss the topic and its meaning. Written rules that encompass a previously developed dictionary are fundamental in identifying themes and directions and can be important to reliability. Nonetheless, latent coding was inherently difficult because of the subjectivity of the respondents. On the other hand, "validity of latent coding can exceed that of manifest coding because people communicate meaning in many implicit ways that depend on context, not just specific words" said Neuman (p.276).

Responses from Round II were analyzed as objective, quantitative data following descriptive statistical analysis for rating of responses. The statistical mean will illustrate the average rating. The standard deviation will show the degree of agreement or lack thereof among Delphi panelists. The quantitative data analysis is the result from the Likert-type scale survey. Since the numerical data resulting from the survey will be categorized as univariate, it will be described and summarized with a frequency distribution. A raw count and a percentage frequency distribution summarized the resulting nominal data (Neuman, 1997).

Data Analyses Technique Selection Appropriateness

For the reasons stated at the onset of this section, this study utilized manifest and latent coding, and information from the responses was annotated on an Excel recording sheet. The combination of these two coding systems strengthened the results. For this study, the units of analysis derived from the review of literature and the research questions. The units of analysis were organized into main broad categories corresponding to the purpose of the questions and survey items: (a) the definition of intuition; and (b) the role of intuition in decision-making.

The coding of the information was performed according to personal judgment. The use of several coders would entail training a strict supervision to insure "consistency across coders and intercoder reliability–a type of equivalence reliability, with a statistical coefficient that tells the degree of consistency among coders" (Neuman, 1997, p.277). Additionally, despite provisions to have research assistants, deviations in coding could still occur, "necessitating retraining and coding the text a second time" (p.277). The time constraints surrounding this study did not render that arrangement feasible.

Neuman (1997) outlined the procedures for what the former termed domain analysis, "an innovative and comprehensive approach for analyzing qualitative data" (p. 429). The systems entails organizing the data units or domains "into taxonomies or broader themes" (p. 429) such as "a term or phrase, a semantic relationship, and included terms" (p. 429). This procedure was the initial process of organizing the data from the first round of responses, into clusters of information. Technically, the process entailed highlighting sections of the text in each case study and assigning a code to the various categories of information. A triage of the information obtained was made; the themes, words, expressions, constructs, and language that were pertinent and significant to the study were separated from the non-relevant. Subsequently, themes were highlighted and coded linked to the information gathered, and the research questions. Data was categorized according to demographic groupings, gender, age, race, and nationality.

Step two entails triaging the data. The various highlighted blocks of information gleaned from organizing the data were categorized into logical groups and subgroups. Semantic relationships or analogies that fall within the domain (Neuman, 1997) were sought. These semantic relationships were drawn from the words themselves, and the similarities and differences were compared. The data was organized into "sets on the basis of logical similarity" (p. 432).

Step 3 involved constructing new ideas and broader themes from the links created (Neuman, 1997). Once the data was arranged in a structured format, the data was reviewed for the conceptual implications and conclusions. The emerging themes, threads of information, expressions, constructs, symbols, and concepts were explored. The expected outcome of the data collection were answers to the basic research questions, and the development of new themes or theories.

Research literature provides copious evidence of the applicability of the Delphi method to this study. In accordance with Adler and Ziglio (1996), there is historical evidence of the Delphi method reliability and flexibility in the investigation of appropriate initiatives, suggestions and concepts for (future) decision-making (Adler & Ziglio, 1996). It has also been employed in the past to "identify major issues" (Mann, 1997, p. 51). Although originally devised for technology forecasting, the Delphi method has expanded beyond that sphere, finding its way into the government, industry and the academia (Fowles, 1978). Furthermore, its flexibility in allowing changes renders it a suitable methodology to explore abstract, complex, and not immediately visible issues as the term Delphi implies (Helmer, 1977; Schmidt, 1995; Mann, 1997). Due to the abstract nature of the questions that structured this study, which required eliciting opinions from a group of experts in the banking field, the Delphi method was deemed as the appropriate methodology.

Following Delbecq et al.'s (1975) advice, prior to establishing whether the Delphi method was the best technique available, thorough considerations about the nature of the population and the milieu within which the method will be applied were made. A number of implications were examined before making the decision of selecting or discarding the Delphi method (Adler and Ziglio, 1996); they were namely: (a) the nature of group communication process most adequate to explore the concept of intuition in decision-making by virtue of the panelists' scarcity of time to meet face to face; (b) the banking experience and seniority of the panelists; (c) the panelists location and mobility; and (d) a cost/benefit ratio analysis. Schmidt (1995) observed that one of the attractive features of the Delphi method is that it allows for the "opportunity to express radical or widely divergent views in a non-threatening context" (p. 139), and for participants to see their own thinking reflected in the responses while learning from others' responses. The satisfactory response to these queries led to the conclusion that the selection of the Delphi was in agreement with the context of the study. Schmidt (1995) noted that the Delphi method must observe three criteria: "(a) Anonymity; (b) iterations and controlled feedback; and (c) statistical group response" (p.127). Echoing Schmidt's views, Linstone & Turoff (2002) emphasized that the Delphi process entails three essential elements that are fundamental: (1) structuring of information flow; (2) feedback to the participants;

and (3) anonymity for the participants. Such characteristics may offer distinct advantages over the conventional face-to-face forum as a communication tool.

Chapter Summary

The main points presented in Chapter 3, addressed the purpose and need for a study about intuition in decision-making to leadership, and the choice of the Delphi method as the appropriate design in view of the abstract and complex nature of intuition in decision-making (Adler & Ziglio, 1996). The intent of the study was to explore the views of 36 geographically dispersed American and Brazilian bankers on the role of intuition in decision-making. The proposed design accomplished this goal by creating a forum where a panel of banking experts anonymously registered and expressed their views. During this process, panelists had the opportunity to refine their opinions, build on them while learning from the responses of others. The summaries of responses underpinned the learning opportunity.

Data collection was carried out in two consecutive and cumulative rounds. A set of open-ended questions designed to discern the expert panel's views, concepts and opinions on intuition constituted the initial instrument of data collection, which was subsequently refined and rebuilt by means of a Likert-type scale survey. The open-ended questions comprised the qualitative aspect of the study while the survey constituted the quantitative segment of the study. The survey was developed based on the initial batch of responses to the open –ended questions. Therefore, data collected was of a qualitative and quantitative nature. Qualitative data analysis was statistically performed based on a combination of manifest and latent coding systems and quantitative data analysis was performed using descriptive statistics. In accordance with Creswell's (2002) guidelines, the first step involved transcribing the data gathered from the open-ended questions. After careful and meticulous reading, this material was organized according to major conceptual themes. The Atlas.ti qualitative data analysis software was utilized to conduct the qualitative analysis. Internal and external validity were ensured by means of dissertation committee members' revisions and suggestions.

As demonstrated throughout this chapter, the threats to validity and reliability of sampling, instrument, and findings were mainly a result of a lack of cross-analysis, poor sampling, illusory expertise, inadequate coding systems, untested data collection instruments and questionnaires, researcher's bias, and manipulation of findings (Martino, 1978). Revisions and critiques provided by the dissertation committee members, pilot testing, and clear guidelines for the coding system were the measures identified to counter these problems.

CHAPTER 4: RESULTS

Increasing market volatility and global uncertainties create challenges for bank leaders and their decision-making processes. Furthermore, the limitations of traditional analytical tools alone hinder the effectiveness of those decisions as well as the use of intuition in foreseeing and dealing with those uncertainties. In search of an answer to this problem, the intent of this non-experimental, qualitative, multi-iterative Delphi study was to describe and conceptualize *the phenomenon of intuition in the decision-making process of 36 American and Brazilian bankers around the world,* employing convenience and snowball sampling strategies. The Delphi design used two data collection procedures to gather information about intuition from a panel of geographically dispersed experts. The Delphi design served the purpose of deepening the understanding of the evolving patterns, responses, or explanations until consensus was possible. The two data collection methods encompassed the following: (a) one to three open-ended questions; and (b) a 5 point Likert-type scale survey (Gall, Borg, & Gall, 2003; Leedy & Omrod, 2001) comprised of 20 questions. The questions and survey items were hosted online by means of a secure and professional, full-featured and streamlined online survey software called Zoomerang, a worldwide renowned online survey software (Zoomerang.com, 2006). The Zoomerang is an Internet-based survey tool that allows researchers to design, program, send, administer surveys, and analyze the results in real time (Zoomerang.com, 2006). This approach was adequate because the process intended to be minimally disruptive or invasive to the participants' daily routine. The data collection process followed a three-round format of the Delphi method of questions combined with summaries of responses that allowed the panelists to learn from one another. The essence of the Delphi method represented a unique research approach to the problem in the way that it allowed access to attitudinal data not normally obtainable from other research activities (Lindstone & Turoff, 2002).

This chapter presents an overview of the data collection procedures, analysis, and interpretation of results of the Delphi Round I and Round II of data collection. Round I represented a qualitative nature and Round II represented a quantitative nature. Round III entailed the presentation of the results to the expert panelists as the utmost contribution and participation were obtained in two rounds. Smith (1995) portrayed the complex and holistic combination of subjective data with numerical data in the Delphi method, as descriptive of a fourth-generation statistical tool. Following Smith's model, textual and pictorial representations illustrate the results for each round.

It is important to elucidate two essential considerations underlying and connecting the rounds of this Delphi study. The first consideration refers to the understanding that the Delphi method is cited in the literature as encompassing a range of one to four rounds before consensus is achieved. Consensus is a concept that causes controversy and ambiguity as it has the connotation of unanimity based on the Hegelian principle that all parties think and act as a unified, undivided whole (Stuter, 1998). Stuter also stated that consensus is an evolutionary process wherein antitheses become synthesis of a new concept. From this point, although consensus is ingrained in the Delphi method of successive rounds, the philosophical approach underlying the Delphi method was rather one of exploration rather than one of unanimity. Bearing in mind that unanimity is seldom reached (Uhlman, 2006); a reasonable degree of stability in the mainstream themes emerging from the responses was observed even though some views remained in the periphery. The second consideration is a corollary to the first consideration, consensus, in the recognition of the understanding that the subjectivity intrinsic to the Delphi methodology and to the panelists' views and perceptions are not extraneous to an exploratory, iterative process.

Pilot Study–Round I

Prior to launching the Delphi study, a trial experiment was conducted with approximately 10% of the population (three panelists)–two Brazilian panelists and one American panelist–to assess the practicability of the Zoomerang survey software, accessible through www. Zoomerang.com. Panelists were invited to evaluate the parameters of confidentiality of the survey site, and the quality of operational procedures. This medium facilitated the customized construction and analysis of qualitative and quantitative surveys to specific target panels. Zoomerang.com is a property of Marketing Tools that offers a full range of survey tools and assistance from the design, plan, and presentation of the survey, keys for survey management, configurations, editions and navigation, anonymous invitation to panelists, timed reminders, visitation and participation rates, visualization of collective and individual responses, and options for shared results or privacy of report generation.

The pilot test proved to be useful. Two panelists were unable to receive the Zoomerang survey invitation, and therefore access the site owing to a strong antivirus protection in their computers. The Zoomerang.com technical support team provided recommendations and solutions to the problem. Based on that technical support information, at the on-set of the study, the panelists were advised to disable their computers' antivirus protection temporarily in order to be able to access the survey site.

Following the pilot test of the survey site, a pilot test of the open-ended questions was conducted. The open-ended questions were submitted to the panelists' individual appraisal. The questions had initially been subject to the dissertation committee members' review. However, the collective opinions, critiques, and suggestions of committee members and panelists were sought to reduce researcher's bias, improve quality of format, pertinence, and depth of questions. The open-ended questions in the pilot study were as follows:

1. How do you define intuition?
2. What role does intuition play in your daily business decision-making?
3. To what extent does intuition play a role in decision-making as it relates to strategy formulation, cost reduction, and performance gaps?

The pilot test for the first round of questions was performed by means of a simultaneous and anonymous deployment of invitations to all the panelists utilizing the www.Zoomerang. com portal for Internet-based professional surveys (Appendix I). Upon accessing the Zoomerang survey site, the panelists saw on the first page a personalized Web greeting that was tailored to the Delphi study. The greeting also requested that panelists review the questions and share their comments and suggestions for improvements. No critiques or comments were offered and panelists commenced to respond to the questions.

The panelists were allotted one week to respond from the time the open-ended questions were presented, but few responded. After three days, notices were sent out via telephone and email to those participants who had not responded to remind them of the approaching deadline for the first round. Nevertheless, despite the initial enthusiasm on the part of the panelists and successive notices and reminders, the response rate was negligible. The timing of the study launch was the cause of the occurrence. The study had been launched on December 1, 2006 coinciding with the end of the fiscal year, the closing of financial statements, and the holiday season. For holiday reasons, more than 60% of the panelists were either unavailable or on vacation, thus causing a significant delay in obtaining immediate feedback. Full participation was achieved only in the middle of January after all panelists had resumed their normal routine. Given the circumstances, the dearth of participation was an unexpected phenomenon.

Analysis of data gathered from the open-ended questions used qualitative data analysis software. The Atlas.ti (Atlas.ti, 2006) constitutes the most recommended qualitative data analysis tool focusing on an interpretational, structural, and reflective analysis. Analysis of the quantitative, survey data used the Zoomerang.com (2006) online survey services, since it provided a level of data analysis that consolidated the survey responses. Zoomerang's (2006) built-in advanced analysis tools processed and analyzed the data gathered from the 5-point Likert-type scale items.

For the purpose of this research study, intuition was defined as "The all-knowing faculty of the soul, which enables man to experience direct perception of truth without the intermediary of the senses"(Yogananda, 2003, p. 458). The metaphor of a direct line with the cosmos is one present in the history of civilization from the thinking of the ancient philosophers to the musings of postmodern thinkers (Smith, 1995; Sowerby, 2001; Moser & van der Nat, 2003; McNaughton, 2003). Goleman (1998) called intuition the "*inner rudder*" (p.51) categorizing it as an important element of emotional intelligence.

Wren (1994) suggested that the definition of decision-making is a human choice, and executive functions comprised of two facets, analysis, and synthesis. Barnard (1942) described analysis and synthesis in the following manner:

> Analysis, or the search for the 'strategic factors' that would create the set, or system of conditions necessary to accomplish the organization's purposes; and synthesis, or the recognition of the interrelationships between elements or parts that together made up the whole system. (p. 271)

The multi-iterative Delphi method was an appropriate design for this study, because the contributions of the Delphi panel helped define reality by giving meaning to thoughts and beliefs (Linstone & Turoff, 2002). The use of a multi-iteration Delphi survey enabled anonymous, systematic refinement of expert opinions with the aim of arriving at a combined or consensual position (Helmer, 1967; Simon 2006). The object of the Delphi method was to obtain a reliable consensus of a group of experts, in this case chief executive bank officers and presidents, by giving them a series of questions and surveys interspersed with controlled opinion feedback (Helmer, 1967; Dalkey, 1969; Delbecq, 1975; Clayton, 1997; Linstone & Turoff, 2002). From this perspective, the Delphi method did not identify dependent relationships or comparisons. The qualitative rationale was an appropriate method to this research study, because it rendered itself to the exploration and description of the use of intuition in the context of a *real life* situation. Given that the purpose of qualitative research was to describe and reveal the rationale of using intuition and verify findings in a *real world* setting (Leedy & Omrod, 2001), the use of intuition in decision-making that occurs in a natural setting was examined and explored.

Organization of Chapter

Consistent with the fact that data for this study were collected by qualitative and quantitative means, results are presented separately reflecting the two methodologies. The qualitative data are presented in narrative and graphic form, whereas tables depict the quantitative data. The review of data collection procedures in this chapter is arranged sequentially into three segments: (a) a pilot test of the survey site, and a pilot test of the three questions for the first round; (b) the sequential order in which the three questions of the qualitative round were presented in the first round; and (c) the representation of the 20 Likert-type scale survey items presented in the second round. The research questions, the Likert-type scale survey items utilized on each round of data collection, as well as, the central themes identified in the responses functioned as the framework for the organization of this chapter. Each theme was described separately, and the frequency with which they were cited in the panelists' responses was graphically illustrated. An overview of the demographic data and research questions is presented, followed by a detailed description of each round, and as a conclusion, a comprehensive summary synthesizes the findings from the two rounds of data collection, thus providing the foundation for a preliminary analysis.

Review of Data Collection Procedures

Utilizing convenience and snowball sampling strategies, 36 bank chief executives were invited to participate as Delphi expert panelists in the survey. Reiterating Clayton (1997) and Westbrook (1997), Uhlman (2006) affirmed that a minimum of 15 panelists would suffice in a reliable Delphi study. The number of panelists invited served as a cautionary measure determined by the time constraints bank executives contend with on a daily basis, which might represent a source of attrition.

The criterion for selection of panelists subscribed to Patton (2001) and Gall et al.'s (2003) recommendation of professionals knowledgeable in the subject of the research. Additional criteria identified as equally essential were: (a) the nationalities of panelists; (b) the accessibility of panelists via email addresses and access to the Internet; (c) the seniority of the panelists' decision-making responsibility and influence; (d) the diversity of job positions and bank areas allowed for higher degree of representation; and (e) the fluency or proficiency in the English language since the research was conducted in this language.

Upon obtaining acceptance and verbal confirmations of the willingness to volunteer to participate in the research study, the Informed Consent Forms were sent electronically, along with the Confidentiality Agreements, and the Demographics Questionnaires to each panelist's individual email address. The panelists were then requested to type their names and responses electronically and to return the forms, as Word documents, to the researcher's University of Phoenix email address. Apart from being more expeditious, electronic delivery, and receipt of the documents provided evidence of panelists' acknowledgement and official participation. From the initial 41 invitees, 33 panelists completed, signed and returned the forms, and later participated in the study.

The methodology utilized in this study followed the guidelines of the Delphi method, which comprised of a total of three rounds conducted online. There were two cumulative and iterative rounds of data collection interspersed with analytical summaries of responses and opinion annotations, and one last round consisting of presentation of results. The first round was of a qualitative nature, and the second round was of a quantitative nature. The first round involved three open-ended questions, and the second round involved 20, 5 point Likert-type scale survey items which were constructed based on two sources: (a) the research frame questions; and (b) the themes that were distilled from the panelists' responses to the open-ended questions.

Preparation for Data Analysis/Preliminary Analyses

From the on-set of this Delphi study, the demographic data collected via the questionnaires evidenced that the panelists embodied a learned faction of professionals in a diverse, albeit, and sophisticated range of positions. The diversity of the panelists extended to the geographic location, age range, and uneven gender division (see table 4). Nonetheless, one commonality bounding the majority of panelists was their educational background, since there was a predominance of graduate degrees (see appendix B).

Although gender and age did not constitute variables in this study, they were portrayed as illustrations. Hsiao (2003) extolling the advantages of panel data, emphasized that panel data indicators may be useful in answering significant questions or explaining phenomena. Table 4 depicts the demographic profile of American panelists who agreed to participate in this study.

Table 4

Panelists' Demographic Information

Panelist	Gender	Age	Country of Origin	Job Function
P1	Male	50-60	United Sates	Vice-President
P2	Male	50-60	Brazil	Global Managing Director
P3	Male	30-40	Brazil	CEO
P4	Female	30-40	Brazil	Vice-President
P5	Male	50-60	United States	CEO
P6	Female	40-50	Brazil	CEO
P7	Male	40-50	Brazil	Credit Director
P8	Male	50-60	United States	Director

P9	Male	50-60	Brazil	CEO
P10	Male	40-50	Brazil	Director Investment
P11	Male	40-50	United States	Senior Vice-President
P12	Male	40-50	United States	Managing Director
P13	Male	50-60	Brazil	Director Operations
P14	Female	40-50	Brazil	Credit Vice-President
P15	Male	40-50	United States	Country Manager
P16	Male	50-60	United States	Senior Vice-President
P17	Female	40-50	United States	Vice-President
P18	Female	40-50	United States	Vice-President
P19	Female	40-50	Brazil	Finance Manager
P20	Male	40-50	Brazil	CEO
P21	Male	40-50	Brazil	Managing Director
P22	Male	40-50	Brazil	Superintendent
P23	Female	40-50	Brazil	CEO
P24	Female	30-40	Brazil	Senior Vice-President
P25	Male	50-60	Brazil	CEO
P26	Female	40-50	United States	Vice-President
P27	Male	40-50	United States	Director
P28	Male	40-50	Brazil	Managing Director
P29	Female	40-50	United States	Assistant Vice-President
P30	Male	50-60	Brazil	Head of Finance
P31	Male	40-50	Brazil	Relationship Director
P32	Male	40-50	Brazil	Managing Director
P33	Male	40-50	Brazil	Branch Manager

The majority (32) of the 33 panelists who participated in the first phase of the study was Native Americans and Brazilians with the exception of panelist number 8 who was naturalized American. This does not imply that they were residing in their countries of origin during the study. All panelists were fully employed at the inception of the study, occupied senior leadership positions, and were considered experts in their respective job areas.

Table 5 depicts the number of males and females who participated in this study.

Table 5

Number of Males and Females

Gender of Panelists	Number of Panelists
Male	13
Female	10

Although gender proportion was not a criterion accented in this study, during the sampling process, repeated and increasing efforts were made to ensure gender equality among panelists. However, the number of referrals for males superseded that of females, regardless of the gender of the person referring or appointing. The number of male panelists might suggest a disparity in the number of females occupying senior positions similar to those occupied by their male counterparts in the banking industry (see appendix B). Table 6 depicts a breakdown of the number of American and Brazilian banking panelists who participated in this study.

Table 6

Breakdown of Panelists According to Nationality

Nationality of Panelists	Number of Panelists
American	11
Brazilian	21
Total	33

The imbalance between the number of American and Brazilian panelists shown in Table 6 was a result from the withdrawal of eight American panelists. The panelists who withdrew from the study did so before the onset of the research process. No reasons were provided for the decision. Table 7depicts a breakdown of the ages and numbers of panelists who participated in this study.

Table 7

Number of Panelists per Age Group

Age of Panelists	Number of Panelists
30-40	5
40-50	20
50-60	8
Total	33

The age of the majority of panelists, approximately 60%, fell in the late forties and late fifties. Although these ages are not an indicator of seniority, as three of the most senior leadership positions, roughly 15% fell within that age bracket (see appendix B). From developmental and career progression perspectives, it was expected that this age range would be a marker of seniority in the population of this study. In contrast, the high percentage of senior leaders in the 30-40 age range represented an unanticipated characteristic in the population sample.

Position titles and nomenclature in the banking industry vary from company to company. In order to facilitate presentation and visualization of the demographics, the diverse panelists' positions were classified into the four following major ranks: (a) CEO; (b) Managing Directors, equivalent to Regional or Global Directors; (c) Directors; (d) Vice – Presidents; and (e) Assistant Vice-Presidents. Table 8 depicts the number of panelists in each of the five positions ranks.

Table 8

Number of Panelists in the Five Position Ranks

Position of Panelists	Number of Panelists
CEO	8
Managing Director	5
Director	5
Vice-President	11
Assistant Vice-President	4
Total	33

Although the position of CEO encompassed the universe of banking leadership positions considered for this study, the number of CEOs (24%) was unexpectedly high, taking into consideration that both personal referral and participation were voluntary. The number of CEOS depicted in Table 7 converges with the numbers presented in Table 6. The low percentage is understandable, since these positions have a regional or global scope and absorb a higher but smaller segment on the corporate pyramid. The number of Managing Directors (15%) equaled the number of Directors (15%), totaling 30% of the panelists. The position most highly represented in this study was that of Vice-President (nearly 33%) a high percentage relative to the CEO, Managing Director, Director, and Assistant Vice-President Positions. Such factors seem fitting with the hierarchy in the banking industry, wherein, the more senior positions become scarcer at the higher levels of the corporate ladder. Panelists in Assistant Vice-President Positions were eligible to participate in this study because they met the requirements of tenure in the banking industry, as well as, the incumbents occupy leadership positions.

Qualitative Data Analysis–Round I

The preparation for a preliminary analysis of data gathered from the open-ended questions *consisted of the following core steps: (a) the attentive reading and summarizing of the responses; (b) the reflective scrutiny of the structural, linguistic and semantic characteristics of the responses; (c)* the creation of a coherent scientific data analysis structure that would accurately discern the themes that surfaced from the responses; and (d) the organization of these views into meaningful and logical categories and patterns. Words, expressions, thoughts, opinions, and concepts that defined intuition and appeared successively were highlighted, organized, and categorized into code groups. Semantic relationships or analogies stemmed from those words that converged under the same semantic domain (Neuman, 1997). For this purpose, content analysis was utilized by means of qualitative data analysis software, Atlas.ti (Atlas.ti, 2006). The software hermeneutic approach to qualitative data interpretation permitted the organization of the responses by the frequency with which certain themes, concepts, and constructs appeared.

Raw data were stored in text format in the Zoomerang software and were later exported in Excel format for analysis. The concepts reflected in the responses were not considered in isolation. Rather, they were counted, and, if mutually corroborating, were regarded as interconnected groups or concept clusters that formed a web of meaning. The themes were comprehensively listed and organized into a table, and classified as units of language according to the rate of recurrence by using the Excel computer feature.

Description of Qualitative Data Analysis

Round I of the Delphi encompassed three questions. The first question asked the panelists to define or describe intuition according to their personal perception and experience. The second question solicited an explanation as to what role intuition played in their decision-making process. The third question probed further on the second question requesting that panelists described what role intuition played on their strategy formulation, cost reduction and performance gap and improvement decision-making. The themes and patterns evolving from the responses to each question (see appendix H) were tabulated (see Table 9), and the number of times they appeared in the responses was scored below:

Table 9

Frequency of Words and Expressions in Question 1: How do you define intuition?

Word/Expression	Frequency
Knowledge or Awareness Without Deliberate Reasoning	24%
Feeling	39%
Based on Past Experience	39%
Not Based on Evidence	15%
Non-Factual	12%
Gut Feeling	12%
Instinct	9%
Insight	9%
Perception of Something	6%
Instinctive	6%
Immediate Decisions	3%
To Realize	3%
Perception of Truth	3%
Direct Perception	3%
Instinctively	3%
Not Based on Logic	3%
Instinctiveness	3%
Subtle Sign	3%
Sixth Sense	3%
Not a Guess	3%
An Art	3%
Unconscious	3%

The textual expressions and phrases that were most frequently used as definitions for intuition were the following: (a) knowledge without deliberate reasoning; (b) instinct; (c) gut feeling; (d) feeling; (d) perception of truth; (e) based on past experience; and (f) insight. Three textual expressions and phrases that emerged less frequently were the following: (a) subtle sign recognition; (b) sixth sense; (c) an unconscious process. Such expressions or constructs were retained verbatim in the elaboration of the codes or units of language, in order to preserve the integrity and veracity of their meaning. Responses from all panelists were taken into account, with the exception of one response because of lack of clarity. Panelist 8 proposed "Sometimes you have an idea that something is wrong and the process needs to be re-examined and then adjusted based on facts within a firm." An attempt to establish a semantic correlation between the words used in the response, and the responses from other panelists, was made, however, no literal expressions equivalent to the words listed on Table 8 were found. In order to avoid discrepancies in the internal coherence of the analysis of responses, the response was disregarded.

In general, respondents employed the listed expressions either concurrently with one another or synonymously. In order to avoid repetitiousness and possible distortions to the data, constructs that were analogous, or related, were merged into a single theme, thus streamlining the list of themes. An elaboration of the rationale for this procedure follows.

The three expressions, instinct, gut feeling, and feeling, appeared simultaneously and were used interchangeably in a significant number of responses. A representative example originated from Panelist 2: "An instinctive form of knowledge (as opposed to formal) a.k.a. gut feeling,", and Panelist 16, who stated that intuition is "an abstract feeling" referred by some as "gut feeling." It made good semantic sense to combine the expressions instinct and feelings together into one single code or unit of language because since they are used synonymously in neurological studies. For example, quoting Müller (1870-1962), Neundörfer and Hilz (1997) placed instinct and feelings, along with other survival instincts in the form of natural tendencies, stored in the brain, as memories and as structures ruled by the limbic system which belongs in the realm of the visceral nervous system.

Panelists 1 and 3 respectively used the following phrases and expressions "knowledge or awareness without deliberate reasoning," and "Perception of truth or fact, etc, independent of any reasoning process," "Intuition is to realize; the perception of something," and "Insight" (see appendix H). These constructs are semantically similar to the unit of language "knowledge without deliberate reasoning" which was extracted verbatim from the response from Panelist 1. The latter is broader in meaning as it encompasses the other two constructs. The basis for this reasoning was that they converge with the following two definitions of intuition examined in the literature review: (a) Jung (1973) who stated that intuition is the ability to understand or know something without resorting to the rationalization process; and (b) Patton (2003) who vaguely equated intuition to a form of insight. For these reasons, the expression "knowledge without deliberate reasoning" was selected as a single theme or code.

The expressions and phrases "subtle sign recognition" from Panelist 5, "sixth sense" from Panelist 17, and "unconscious" stated by Panelist 20 were used only once in each response (see Appendix H) and these expressions and phrases were analyzed separately. For the purposes of effectiveness and clarity of data analysis, the resulting codes used can be described as the following three main units of language: (a) instinct, gut feeling, and feelings; (b) knowledge without deliberate reasoning/perception of truth/insight; and (c) information based on past experience.

The instinctual and emotional characteristics of intuition were the most frequently mentioned and distinguishing feature (41%), (see Figure 2). This instinctual and emotional characteristic was reflected in the use of such expressions as the following: "intuition is when you feel that pursuing a certain objective is the right thing to do" or "instinctive knowing" (see appendix H). Phrases with implicit emotional overtones included the following: "intuition is a feeling if something good or bad could happen," "abstract feeling," and "inexplicable conviction" (see appendix H). Figure 2 below illustrates the frequency in which each unit of language occurred:

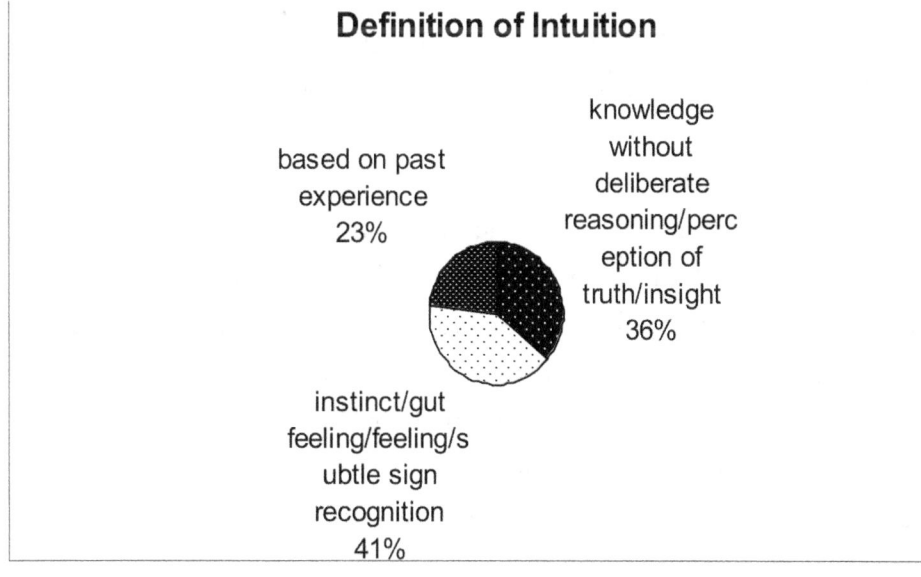

Figure 2. Definition of intuition.

The theme cluster knowledge without deliberate reasoning/perception of truth/insight emerged in 36% of the responses and corresponded to Chaui's (2003) description of intuition as *a complete and immediate comprehension of an entity, or fact, exclusive of verification or substantiation. Additionally, the themes alluded to the transcendental quality of intuitive thinking often found in Jung's explanations. By way of semantics, the themes suggested a holistic dimension of intuition that integrates the rational and creative capabilities echoing Garmston's (2006) views.*

Definitions of intuition also appeared in the responses in connection with past experiences. Such descriptions compose 23% of the responses (see Figure 2). Panelists stated that intuition was the ability to perceive "signs born from experience" or emerging from one's own "set of collective experiences." An additional thought pertained to the accumulation of "registered information, experiences" as the fundaments of intuition. Another panelist said that intuition was "insight gained from historical experience." Within this same theme, there were references made to subtle sign recognition and the unconscious.

Panelist 5 described intuition as comparative to "the ability to recognize subtle signs." The panelist commented that this recognition is "born from experience," and it "can affect decision making." This argument is akin to other panelists' description of intuition as resulting from experience; but, conversely, it introduced the unprecedented concept of being aware of and identifying symbols, messages, patterns, or situations that are not overt or not apparent to others. Although, at a first glance, it seems to contradict other panelists' assertions, subtle sign recognition is a function of memory. The panelist further attested that intuition in "an instinct born from experience making a link between recognition and instinctual component of human behavior and thus establishing a relationship between the two.

A similar style in responding to the first question was found in the connection with the unconscious mind. Panelist 20 made the case that intuition is an "unconscious thinking process," that it is "unique to the individual." The response stood out for its apparent dichotomy linking the word unconscious and thinking. While the act of thinking pertains to the domain of the conscious mind (Khatri & Ng, 2000), the amount of stored information in the unconscious portion of the mind lies beneath the immediate awareness and therefore is inaccessible. Resolution to this issue was offered by the panelists' contention that the unconscious thinking is a process "which consists of the application of a number of that individual's past experiences."

An association with the sixth sense was derived as described in the theme below. There appears to have been no explicitly expressed points of view from other respondents that would corroborate their substance and significance. Descriptions from other respondents differed in opposing ways. Nonetheless, the importance of the concept to the study of intuition is highlighted continually throughout the literature. This contention entreats the need to delve deeper beneath the surface of the themes in order to discern their underlying meaning and implications.

The connection between intuition and a sixth sense was expressed in one particular response where Panelist 17 stated that the "sixth sense" allows information processing. The statement seems to insinuate that there is an affinity between intuition and a paranormal or metaphysical ability. It is important to stress, nonetheless, that in the same response the panelist included a reference to a rational activity by using the words "it allows one to assimilate various data points." There was another concept in that panelist's response that can support the conclusion that the panelist appreciated the fact that the "sixth sense" used here interchangeably with intuition, is a broader faculty that enables one "to reach a conclusion that may not be obvious from a single observation."

As regards question two, panelists' responses varied greatly not only in terms of the expressions but also in terms of interpretation to the question. Words and expressions that emerged in question 2 were: "gives me the initial feeling," "minor role," "none," "very little," "do not use," "should be based on data and analysis," "occasionally," "useful role," "semi-annually and annually," "not a major role," "plays a role," "meaningful," "major role," "often /frequent," "on a daily basis," "significant," "huge role," "key factor," "100% of the time," "most of the time," "extremely important," and "final decision factor." Panelists 1, 5, 6,8,13, 19, and 21 responded from a time perspective while the remainders individually used different expressions. For the sake of clarity in data analysis, and to aid in the development of the survey items, the words were grouped under homonymous semantic clusters or units of language according to the frequency in which they occurred. Three units of language resulted in the following: (a) significant; (b) sporadic; and (c) minimal. Table 10 depicted the frequency of words and expressions emerging in question 2.

Table 10

Frequency of Words and Expressions in Question 2.

Words/Expressions	Frequency
Significant	52%
Sporadic	30%
Minimal	18%

In determining the role that intuition plays in the panelists' daily business decision-making, three levels of intensity and regularity were observed from which three themes were subsequently derived. The first theme was the role of intuition was significant in decision-making, representative of a high level of reliance and use of intuition. The second theme was the role of intuition was sporadic in decision-making– indicating that panelists allow intuition to guide their decisions less frequently and as a supplement to numerical and factual information. The third theme was the role of intuition was minimal in decision-making–denoting that intuition is either rarely used or not regarded as useful.

The majority of responses (52%), as demonstrated in Figure 3 below, indicated that intuition has a significant impact on the panelists' decision-making. Such aspect was reflected in the employment of terms that included often, frequent, once a week, meaningful, significant, and key factor. Responses that explicitly articulated and conveyed the idea of intuition playing a central role in the panelists' daily decision making contained the following phrases: "it is a differential in achieving a good balance between risk and return of a portfolio"; "I use it 100% of the time"; "an extremely important one"; "it plays an important role"; and "it is a constant factor in decision-making."

Intuition in Daily Decision-Making

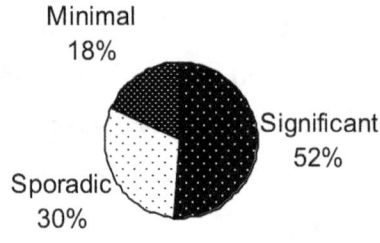

Figure 3. Intuition in daily decision-making.

In the words of the panelists who comprised this group, not only does intuition help but also it is "at the heart of decisions." This contingent overtly stated that intuition is a determinant factor particularly in periods or "situations of uncertainty." Another common theme that emerged was the use of intuition in business interpersonal relationships. An evidence of that idea was the response of two panelists who affirmed that intuition plays a huge role in the interpersonal aspects of their jobs. Analysis of the panel data revealed that panelists who expressed having a high level of reliance and use of intuition in decision-making had two characteristics in common: (a) they occupied the most senior positions; and (b) they held investment or marketing positions.

Panelists who, to a lesser extent, resort to or rely on intuitive thinking when making decisions encompassed 30% of the total population. Phrases embodying that concept included "we try to put as much factual data into a situation as we possibly can;" "we have a lot more focus on facts and data today than we ever have before in our decision making;" and "process has to be based on objective, measurable information." A common comment that surface from panelists was that while their work and decisions do not have a primary focus on intuition, "intuition plays a role." In this contingent intuition was regarded as "a differential" though emphasis is placed on factual data, especially in credit decisions. Further, intuition in those instances was only used in circumstances involving meetings with clients.

The minimal use of intuition was the third level detected in the responses. Eighteen percent of panelists stated that it is tangentially connected to their decision-making. Phrases representative of this theme included "Normally, I do not make decisions by intuition. However, a bit of intuition is always necessary in order to beat the competition;" "very little, if any;" and "hard to tell." Panelists who rarely or minimally rely on intuition acknowledged that "intuition can help one to differentiate from competitors by finding unexplored market niches or anticipating trends" but, in the same manner as the other banking credit panelists who sporadically utilize intuition, they strive instead to "be as analytical as possible when making decisions in regard to credit risk issues". An example of that concept was the phrase "a major part of the decision-making process has to be based on objective, measurable information."

Question three probed further and queried participants for more detail into the role of intuition in the decision-making pertaining to specific financial charges, namely strategy formulation, cost reduction and performance gaps. For the purposes of consistency and efficiency in data analysis, the same levels of intensity and frequency of the use of intuition in decision-making were maintained. The themes are respectively: (a) significant; (b) sporadic; and (c) minimal. Table 11 illustrates the frequency in which the words and expressions occurred. A description of the results follows.

Table 11

Frequency of Words and Expressions Used in Question 3.

Words/Expressions	Frequency
Significant	41%
Sporadic	24%
Minimal	35%

The preponderance of the responses (41%), as demonstrated in Figure 4 below, indicated that panelists rely on intuition in their strategic decisions. Although this figure is representative of the majority of responses, it corresponds to an 11% plunge from the 52% demonstrated in question 2.

Intuition in Strategy Formulation, Cost Reduction and Performance Gaps

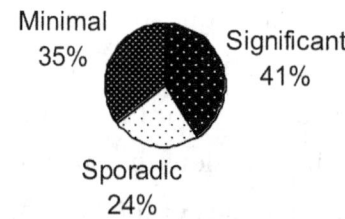

Figure 4. Intuition in strategy formulation, cost reduction and performance gaps.

The broad scope of question 2 may be one explanation for the high percentage in the responses, perhaps denoting that when reading the question, some panelists may have interpreted it as referring to decision-making in general terms. An additional reason may be that the difference between the two questions, specifically, the more pointed wording and reach of question two, could have caused the panelists to rethink and revisit their previous statements. A further possibility might be that question three extends beyond question two, since both have common characteristics. The overlap may have prevented panelists from preserving the same frame of thought to their responses to question two. Nonetheless, the decline in percentage was a surprising finding since all three questions were displayed simultaneously on the survey website, allowing panelists to readily see all three questions at once, note the difference and make judgments about the responses.

Panelists who attributed a significant role to intuition in their decision-making were vocal in mentioning, "intuition helps strategic decisions regarding ways to close gaps or identify emerging opportunities." Panelist 5 commented that intuition plays a large role and protects him "from blunders," helping him "anticipate error." Further, the same panelist held the view that intuition "points out areas to investigate or re-confirm." Additionally, panelist 12 asserted that intuition is instrumental in "formulating the strategic direction and areas of focus of my business unit." Panelist 14 made the case that "intuition helps me to anticipate my own weaknesses when dealing with something new." This view was corroborated by the idea formulated by Panelist 23 that intuition is "a way of broadening strategic decisions as it brings another view on the process." Panelist 7 argued that although information is equally "available in real time to every player," responses to situations very considerably and decisions are "deeply influenced by intuition in the daily routine." A holistic perspective that accepts intuition in the numerical and the interpersonal aspects of decision-making was offered by panelist 6 that is depicted in the phrase "when it comes to strategy, I try to use the intuition as a tool in connection with the client figures, to help us to understand our Client needs and challenges, than we will avoid to take wrong decisions regarding risk level."

Respondents who considered intuition less significant and therefore were not so consistent in their use of it corresponded to 35% of the population. Here there was a 5% increase over the 30% in question two. Again, it is hypothesized that those panelists may have reconsidered their responses or elaborated them. This contingent described their use of intuition in relation to it playing an ancillary role. Such a concept was best expressed by the phrase of Panelist 9 who stated that intuition takes a "secondary role when facts alone are no longer relevant to the process." In corroboration to the notion of intuition as a supplement to decision-making, common themes emerging from responses to this question encompassed expressions such as "much more hard data" (Panelist 18); "less intuition and more hard facts" (Panelist 18); and "there must be a rationale behind every decision" (Panelist 24).

A negligible correlation between intuition and financial decision-making was observed in 24% of the responses, which comprised the minority of the responses. A considerable fraction of this percentage was comprised of words like "none" (Panelist 13); "almost none" (Panelist 20); and "limited" (Panelist 10). The concepts were more amply put across in the phrase from Panelist 19: "in my particular role, intuition can't help me in financial matters but it can help in having the right information at the correct time which can help others in obtaining profits, performances and sometimes even losses."

The role of intuition in decision-making pertaining strategy formulation and cost reductions was not clearly stated in most responses. There was one noteworthy exception where Panelist 26 pronounced, "some level intuition is always involved but possibly to a lesser extent for strategic decisions related to profit, cost losses and performance gaps." That concern was further elaborated in a single say by the panelist who raised the vision that "for this type of decision making process, intuition could play a role in idea generation, when trying to define different ways or specific attributes/factors." According to Panelist 26, intuition would play a limited role and would only have value if it "could be used to analyze and reach the targeted strategic decision."

Quantitative Data Analysis–Round II

The quantitative phase of the Delphi study comprised a Likert-type scale survey containing 20 items. The survey was planned and devised with basis on the panelists' responses to the qualitative phase. The procedural decision to preserve the themes that emerged from the responses in the manner with which the panelists originally wrote them was undertaken in order to minimize researcher bias that might lead the panelists to respond in one pre-determined way (Salkind, 2003). Thus, the themes formed the raw material with which the scalable survey items were developed. A five-point arbitrary scale was designed to collect data and the purpose was three-fold: (a) to deepen the understanding of the panelists' perceptions of the role of intuition in decision-making; (b) to allow the panelists the opportunity to either revisit or confirm the assertions made in the previous phase; and (c) to maximize the chances of obtaining a preponderance of responses to any particular aspect of intuition thus propitiating the generation of a consensus.

In keeping with the purpose of the study, namely to hone panelists' perceptions to intuition, its role in their daily decision-making, and in strategy formulation, cost reduction and performance gaps, the survey items reflected the themes found in the responses to Round I. Additionally, survey items were designed based on the framework research questions and the review of literature. The questions in Round I as well as the research questions guiding the development of survey items are displayed simultaneously with the survey items.

Question 1 from Round I: How do you define intuition?

Framework research questions 5 and 6 used to develop survey item: What are American leaders' views, beliefs, and attitudes regarding the nature of intuition? What are Brazilian bank leaders' views, beliefs, and attitudes regarding the nature of intuition? The following seven survey items were designed using these two questions in combination with the core themes emerging from the panelists' responses to further probe and refine on their definition of intuition.

Survey Items 1: Intuition is a feeling. Table 12 depicts the percentage of responses to this survey item.

Table 12

Distribution of Responses to Survey Item 1

Indicators	Aggregated Responses	Percentage
Not Sure	1	4%
Strongly Disagree	0	0%
Disagree	4	16%
Agree	10	40%
Strongly Agree	10	40%
Total	25	100%

One participant was not sure (4%). Null response (0%) indicated that none of the panelists strongly disagreed that intuition is a feeling. Four panelists (16%) disagreed with the statement. Ten panelists (40%) agreed that intuition is a feeling. Ten panelists (40%) strongly agreed that intuition is a feeling.

Survey Item 2: Intuition is an instinct based on past experience. Table 13 depicts the percentage of responses to this survey item.

Table 13

Distribution of Responses to Survey Item 2

Indicators	Aggregated Responses	Percentage
Not Sure	3	12%
Strongly Disagree	0	0%
Disagree	2	8%
Agree	13	52%
Strongly Agree	7	28%
Total	25	100%

Three panelists (12%) were not sure if intuition is an instinct based on experience. None of the panelists (0%) strongly disagreed with the statement. Two panelists (8%)

disagreed. Thirteen panelists (13%) agreed with the statement. Seven panelists (28%) strongly agreed that intuition is an instinct based on experience.

Survey item 3. Intuition is an irrational, unconscious process. Table 14 depicts the percentage of responses to this survey item.

Table 14

Distribution of Responses to Survey Item 3

Indicators	Aggregated Responses	Percentage
Not Sure	0	0%
Strongly Disagree	7	28%
Disagree	14	56%
Agree	4	16%
Strongly Agree	0	0%
Total	25	100%

There was null response for the survey indicator *not sure.* Seven panelists (28%) strongly disagreed that intuition is an irrational, unconscious process. Fourteen panelists (56%) disagreed that intuition is an irrational, unconscious process. Four panelists (16%) agreed with the statement. Responses to the survey indicator *strongly agree* were null (0%).

Survey item 4: Intuition is the direct, instantaneous and integrated apprehension of truth. Table 15 depicts the percentages of responses to this survey item.

Table 15

Distribution of Responses to Survey Item 4.

Indicators	Aggregated Responses	Percentage
Not Sure	2	8%
Strongly Disagree	1	4%
Disagree	7	28%
Agree	14	56%
Strongly Agree	1	4%
Total	25	100%

Two panelists (8%) were not sure whether intuition is the direct, instantaneous and integrated apprehension of truth. One panelist (4%) strongly disagreed. Seven panelists (28%) disagreed. Fourteen panelists (56%) agreed. One panelist (4%) strongly agreed.

Survey item 5: Intuition is a legitimate decision-making tool utilized by leaders in a myriad of business circumstances. Table 16 depicts the percentages of responses to this survey item.

Table 16

Distribution of Responses to Survey Item 5.

Indicators	Aggregated Responses	Percentage
Not Sure	1	4%
Strongly Disagree	0	0%
Disagree	4	16%
Agree	11	44%
Strongly Agree	9	36%
Total	25	100%

One panelist (4%) was not sure whether intuition is a legitimate decision-making tool utilized by leaders in a myriad of business circumstances. No panelists (0%) strongly disagreed with the statement. Four panelists (16%) disagreed. Eleven panelists (44%) agreed with the statement. Nine panelists (36%) strongly agreed.

Survey item 6: Intuition is a paranormal, irrational phenomenon. Table 17 depicts the percentages of responses to this survey item.

Table 17

Distribution of Responses to Survey Item 6

Indicators	Aggregated Responses	Percentage
Not Sure	0	0%
Strongly Disagree	11	44%
Disagree	11	44%
Agree	1	4%
Strongly Agree	2	8%
Total	25	100%

None of the panelists was sure whether intuition is a paranormal, irrational phenomenon. Eleven panelists (44%) strongly disagreed. Eleven panelists (44%) disagreed with the statement. One panelist (4%) agreed with the statement. Two panelists (8%) strongly agreed.

Survey 7: Intuition is a rational, logical activity stemming from the realm of the inner wisdom. Table 18 depicts the percentages of responses to this survey item.

Table 18

Distribution of Responses to Survey Item 7

Indicators	Aggregated Responses	Percentage
Not Sure	2	8%
Strongly Disagree	0	0%
Disagree	4	16%
Agree	16	64%
Strongly Agree	3	12%
Total	25	100%

Two panelists (8%) were not sure whether intuition is a rational, logical activity stemming from the realm of the inner wisdom. Responses to option *strongly disagree* were null (0%). Four panelists (16%) disagreed with the statement. Sixteen panelists (64%) agreed with the statement. Three panelists strongly (12%) agreed.

Question 2 from Round II: What role does intuition play in your daily decision-making?

Survey Item 8: The role of intuition in my decision-making process can be best described as Minimal. The following seven survey items were designed using these two questions in combination with the core themes emerging from the panelists' responses to further probe and refine. Table 19 depicts the percentage of responses to this survey item.

Table 19

Distribution of Responses to Survey Item 8

Indicators	Aggregated Responses	Percentage
Not Sure	0	0%
Strongly Disagree	6	24%

Disagree	14	56%
Agree	4	16%
Strongly Agree	1	4%
Total	25	100%

None of the panelists (0%) was sure whether the role of intuition in decision-making process could be best described as Minimal. Six panelists (24%) strongly disagreed with the statement. Four panelists (16%) agreed with the statement. One panelist (4%) strongly agreed with the statement.

Survey item 9: The role of intuition in my decision-making process can be best described as Sporadic. Table 20 depicts the percentage of responses to this survey item.

Table 20

Distribution of Responses to Survey Item 9

Indicators	Aggregated Responses	Percentage
Not Sure	0	0%
Strongly Disagree	2	8%
Disagree	11	44%
Agree	9	36%
Strongly Agree	3	12%
Total	25	100%

Survey item 10: The role of intuition in my decision-making process can be best described as significant. Table 21 depicts the percentage of responses to this survey item.

Table 21

Distribution of Responses to Survey Item 10

Indicators	Aggregated Responses	Percentage
Not Sure	0	0%
Strongly Disagree	1	4%
Disagree	10	40%
Agree	12	48%
Strongly Agree	2	8%
Total	25	100%

None of the panelists (0%) was sure whether the role of intuition in decision-making process could be best described as significant. One panelist (4%) strongly agreed with the statement. Ten (40%) disagreed with the statement. Twelve panelists (48%) agreed with the statement. Two panelists (8%) strongly agreed.

Survey item 11: I favor intuitive thinking in my decision-making process. Table 22 depicts the percentage of responses to this survey item.

Table 22

Distribution of Responses to Survey Item 11

Indicators	Aggregated Responses	Percentage
Not Sure	2	8%
Strongly Disagree	1	4%
Disagree	11	44%
Agree	9	36%
Strongly Agree	2	8%
Total	25	100%

Two panelists (8%) were not sure whether they favor intuitive thinking in decision-making process. One panelist (4%) strongly disagreed with the statement. Eleven panelists (44%) disagreed with the statement. Nine panelists (36%) agreed with the statement. Two panelists (8%) strongly agreed with the statement.

Survey item 12: I favor logical and rational reasoning in my decision-making process. Table 23 depicts the percentage of responses to this survey item.

Table 23

Distribution of Responses to Survey Item 12

Indicators	Aggregated Responses	Percentage
Not Sure	0	0%
Strongly Disagree	0	0%
Disagree	2	8%
Agree	18	72%
Strongly Agree	5	20%
Total	25	100%

None of the panelists (0%) was sure whether they favor logical and rational reasoning in decision-making process. None of the panelists (0%) strongly disagreed with the statement. Two panelists (8%) disagreed with the statement. Eighteen panelists (72%) agreed with the statement. Five panelists (20%) strongly agreed with the statement.

Question 3 from Round I: What role does intuition play in your decision-making processes related to strategy formulation, cost reduction and performance gaps?

Framework research question used to develop survey items: In which decision-making business circumstances do American and Brazilian bank leaders prefer to rely on intuition?

Survey item 13: I rely on intuition in personnel-related business circumstances. Table 24 depicts the percentage of responses to this survey item.

Table 24

Distribution of Responses to Survey Item 13

Indicators	Aggregated Responses	Percentage
Not Sure	0	0%
Strongly Disagree	0	0%
Disagree	9	36%
Agree	14	56%
Strongly Agree	2	8%
Total	25	100%

None of the panelists (0%) was sure whether they rely on intuition in personnel-related business circumstances. There was no response (0%) as to whether the panelists strongly disagreed with the statement. Nine panelists (36%) disagreed with the statements. Fourteen panelists (56%) agreed with the statement. Two panelists (8%) strongly agreed with the statement.

Survey item 1: I rely on intuition in strategic decision-making circumstances. Table 25 depicts the percentage of responses to this survey item.

Table 25

Distribution of Responses to Survey Item 14

Indicators	Aggregated Responses	Percentage
Not Sure	0	0%
Strongly Disagree	0	0%
Disagree	13	52%
Agree	10	40%
Strongly Agree	2	8%
Total	25	100%

None of the panelists (0%) was sure whether they rely on intuition in strategic decision-making circumstances. None of the panelists (0%) strongly disagreed with the statement. Thirteen panelists (52%) disagreed with the statement. Ten (40%) agreed with the statement. Two panelists (8%) strongly agreed with the statement.

Survey item 15: I rely on intuition to determine business performance gaps. Table 26 depicts the percentage of responses to this survey item.

Table 26

Distribution of Responses to Survey Item 15

Indicators	Aggregated Responses	Percentage
Not Sure	1	4%
Strongly Disagree	1	4%
Disagree	18	72%
Agree	4	16%
Strongly Agree	1	4%
Total	25	100%

One panelist (4%) was not sure about relying on intuition to determine business performance gaps. One panelist strongly disagreed with the statement. Eighteen panelists (72%) disagreed with the statement. Four panelists (16%) agreed with the statement. One panelist (4%) strongly agreed with the statement.

Survey item 16: I rely on intuition when assessing market, economic and political scenarios. Table 27 depicts the percentage of responses to this survey item.

Table 27

Distribution of Responses to Survey Item 16

Indicators	Aggregated Responses	Percentage
Not Sure	1	4%
Strongly Disagree	1	4%
Disagree	15	60%
Agree	7	28%
Strongly Agree	1	4%
Total	25	100%

One panelist (4%) was not sure whether intuition was determinant when assessing market, economic and political scenarios. One panelist (4%) strongly disagreed with the statement. Fifteen panelists (60%) disagreed with the statement. Seven panelists (28%) agreed with the statements. One panelist (4%) strongly agreed with the statement.

Survey item 17: Intuition strongly impacts my decision-making on cost reduction and performance improvement.

Table 28 depicts the percentage of responses to this survey item.

Table 28

Distribution of Responses to Survey Item 17

Indicators	Aggregated Responses	Percentage
Not Sure	0	0%
Strongly Disagree	2	8%
Disagree	15	60%
Agree	7	28%
Strongly Agree	1	4%
Total	25	100%

None of the panelists (0%) was sure whether intuition strongly affects decision-making on cost reduction and performance improvement. Two panelists (8%) strongly disagreed with the statement. Fifteen panelists (60%) disagreed with the statement. Seven panelists (28%) agreed with the statement. One panelist (4%) strongly agreed with the statement.

Framework research question 7 used to develop survey item: What benefits do American and Brazilian bank leaders gain from using intuition in decision-making as opposed to traditional fact-based decision-making?

Survey item 18: In my experience, I believe I reap benefits from using intuition in decision-making as opposed to traditional fact-based decision-making. Table 29 depicts the percentage of responses to this survey item.

Table 29

Distribution of Responses to Survey Item 18

Indicators	Aggregated Responses	Percentage
Not Sure	2	8%
Strongly Disagree	0	0%
Disagree	14	56%
Agree	7	28%
Strongly Agree	2	8%
Total	25	100%

Two panelists (8%) stated not being sure as to whether they reap benefits from using intuition in decision-making as opposed to traditional fact-based decision-making. None of the respondents (0%) strongly disagreed. Fourteen panelists (56%) disagreed with the statement. Seven panelists (28%) agreed with the statement. Two panelists (8%) strongly agreed with the statement.

Framework research question used to develop survey item 19: What are the American and Brazilian bank leaders' perceptions of the interrelationship between intuition and decision-making?

Survey item 19: Given the new levels of complexity in decision-making, there is a growing interrelationship between intuition and logical reasoning in decision-making. Table 30 depicts the percentage of responses to this survey item.

Table 30

Distribution of Responses to Survey Item 19

Indicators	Aggregated Responses	Percentage
Not Sure	1	4%
Strongly Disagree	0	0%
Disagree	2	8%
Agree	17	68%
Strongly Agree	5	20%
Total	25	100%

One panelist (4%) indicated not being sure whether given the new levels of complexity in decision-making, and the discoveries of the magnitude of the human cognition, there is a growing interrelationship between intuition and logical reasoning in decision-making. None of the respondents (0%) strongly disagreed with the statement. Two panelists (8%) disagreed with the statement. Seventeen panelists (68%) agreed with the statement. Five panelists (20%) strongly agreed with the statement.

Survey item 20: Corporations ought to encourage the formal development of intuitive thinking to enhance decision-making. Table 31 depicts the percentage of responses to this survey item.

Table 31

Distribution of Responses to Survey Item 20

Indicators	Aggregated Responses	Percentage
Not Sure	3	12%
Strongly Disagree	0	0%
Disagree	8	32%
Agree	8	32%
Strongly Agree	6	24%
Total	25	100%

Three panelists (12%) indicated not being sure as to whether corporations ought to encourage the formal development of intuitive thinking to enhance decision-making. None of the panelists (0%) strongly disagreed with the statement. Eight panelists (32%)

disagreed with the statement. Eight panelists (32%) agreed with the statement. Six panelists (24%) strongly agreed with the statement.

Description of Quantitative Data Analysis

The use of the Delphi method inevitably brings to fore the issue of consensus. Firstly because consensus lies at the heart of the technique; and secondly, owing to the expectation that the level of consensus will augment as the rounds progress from one to the next (Dick, 2000). Vela (1989) stated that accepted ways of verifying consensus include a 50% common response. Concerning this study, it is important to place consensus in its proper perspective, that is, in Gilsford's (1986-1998) words, it seldom occurs. Therefore, bearing in mind that the aim of this Delphi study was to explore and glean information on the views of a panel of banking panelists, the objective was neither to reach a definite position nor to find a resolution to a problem, but to use consensus as a means to ascertain and present the majority of opinions, perceptions and thoughts. These considerations are important given that percentages of responses varied from question two to question three and from Round I to Round II. Further, six panelists withdrew from the study thus reducing the numbers of panelists from 32 in Round I to 24 in Round II. Additionally, the choice to consider responses representative of minority positions created the opportunity to polarize and contrast the diversity of opinions and was instrumental in understanding their influence over the use of intuition on decision-making.

The five alternative indicators were created having in mind the Guttman scaling (Neuman, 1997) and the numerical continuum included *not sure* = 1; *strongly disagree* = 2; *disagree* = 3; *agree* = 4; *and strongly agree* = 5. Researchers debate the use of neutral options (Neuman, 1997). However, the choice to include the alternative *not sure* in the scale was to avoid forcing the respondent into taking a position. Limiting the four alternatives to range from strongly disagreeing at the end of the spectrum through strongly agreeing at the other extreme might lead to data askew since the panelist would be constrained to choose either *agree, strongly agree, disagree or strongly disagree*. By doing so, the panelist might be led to express a premature thought that had not had time to mature. A possible corollary might be the heightening of the risk of committing a breach in the analysis of data.

Additionally, statistical results would not be a truthful representation of panelists' thoughts, and would violate the ethical directives and exigencies of scientific research. The survey categories or indicators *strongly disagree, disagree, agree and strongly agree* were designed to avoid the pitfall of creating a crude measure and forceful distinctions (Neuman, 1997). By increasing the number of options, panelists were able to express their range of views. The five resulting indicators fell in the middle of the 4 to 8 range recommended by Neuman.

Nonetheless, the statistical results to the survey posed a conundrum. In the survey items 1, 6, 12, 13, 14, 15, 16, 18, and 20, the percentages were distributed evenly and panelists' responses were equal, thus creating an impasse. In those survey items, the number of panelists' responses was equivalent for categories *strongly disagree* and *disagree*, and *agree* and *strongly agree*. In order to increase accuracy of data analysis, the four categories *strongly disagree* and *disagree*, and *agree* and *strongly agree* were coalesced into two distinct categories, after the data were collected (Neuman, 1997). Towards that, the categories *strongly disagree* and *strongly agree* collapsed. Two new constructs emerged, *agree* and *disagree*, reflecting the same attitude indicators (p.161). The underlying reason for this procedure was threefold: (a) to avoid the problem of *response set* or *response bias* (p.161) since there was no way to determine from the multiple indicators whether the responses mirrored an attitude, a habit, or a tendency to agree with the question; (b) to fix the panelists' position into one single judgment; and (c) to allow for a more exact comparison among different responses. Modification of scale indicators after survey items are measured is a statistically sound procedure or intervention from the point of view of research ethics and reliability.

The number of panelists participating in Round II decreased from that of Round I (33 panelists). With eight panelists withdrawing from the study during the quantitative data collection in Round II, the total number amounted to 25 panelists – 14 Brazilian panelists and 11 American panelists respectively. Table 32 depicts the demographics of panelists in Round II.

Table 32

Demographics of Panelists in Round II

Nationality of Panelists	Number of Panelists	Percentage
American	11	44%
Brazilian	14	56%

Table 33 depicts the comparison between the responses from American panelists and those of Brazilian panelists. Table 33 illustrates how the combined indicators *agree* and *disagree* (in addition to the neutral *not sure*) determined more clearly the contrast among the three attitudes, drawing attention to the two attitudes. An analysis of each survey item follows.

Table 33

Comparison between American and Brazilian Leaders' Responses.

Bank Leaders	Not Sure	Disagree	Agree
	Intuition is a feeling		
American	0%	12%	32%
Brazilian	8%	8%	40%
	Intuition is a feeling based on experience.		
American	4%	0%	40%
Brazilian	8%	8%	40%
	Intuition is an irrational, unconscious process		
American	0%	36%	8%
Brazilian	0%	44%	12%
	Intuition is the direct, instantaneous and integrated apprehension of truth.		
American	0%	20%	24%
Brazilian	8%	8%	40%
	Intuition is a legitimate decision-making tool utilized by leaders in a myriad of business circumstances.		
American	0%	8%	36%
Brazilian	4%		44%

Table 33 (continued)

Comparison between American and Brazilian Leaders' Responses

Bank Leaders	Not Sure	Disagree	Agree
	Intuition is a paranormal, irrational phenomenon.		
American	0%	44%	0%
Brazilian	0%	56%	0%
	Intuition is a rational, logical activity stemming from the realm of the inner wisdom.		
American	0%	4%	40%
Brazilian	8%	8%	40%
	The role of intuition in my decision-making process can be best described as minimal.		
American	0%	40%	4%
Brazilian	0%	40%	16%
	The role of intuition in my decision-making can be best described as sporadic.		
American	0%	28%	16%
Brazilian	0%	24%	32%
	The role of intuition can be best described as significant.		
American	0%	12%	28%
Brazilian	0%	28%	32%

Table 33 (continued)

Comparison between American and Brazilian Leaders' Responses

Bank Leaders	Not Sure	Disagree	Agree
	I favor intuitive thinking in my business decision-making.		
American	4%	24%	16%
Brazilian	4%	16%	36%
	I favor logical, rational reasoning in my decision-making process.		
American	0%	8%	56%
Brazilian	0%	0%	36%
	In my experience, I believe I reap benefits from using intuition in decision-making as opposed to traditional fact-based decision-making.		
American	0%	32%	12%
Brazilian	0%	36%	20%
	I rely on intuition in personnel-related business circumstances.		
American	0%	24%	24%
Brazilian	0%	16%	36%
	I rely on intuition in strategic decision-making.		
American	0%	24%	24%
Brazilian	0%	16%	36%

Table 33 (continued)

Comparison between American and Brazilian Leaders' Responses

Bank Leaders	Not Sure	Disagree	Agree
	I rely on intuition to determine business performance gaps.		
American	0%	24%	20%
Brazilian	0%	28%	28%
	I rely on intuition when assessing market, economic and political scenarios.		
American	0%	36%	4%
Brazilian	8%	36%	16%
	Intuition strongly impacts my decision-making on cost reduction and performance improvements.		
American	4%	28%	12%
Brazilian	8%	36%	20%
	Given the new levels of complexity in decision-making, there is a growing interrelationship between intuition and logical reasoning in decision-making.		
American	4%	4%	36%
Brazilian	0%	4%	52%

Table 33 (continued)

Comparison between American and Brazilian Leaders' Responses

Bank Leaders	Not Sure	Disagree	Agree
	Corporations ought to encourage the formal development of intuitive thinking to enhance decision-making.		
American	8%	12%	24%
Brazilian	4%	20%	32%

Intuition is a feeling. The majority of the American panelists (32%) agreed that intuition is a feeling, and 12% disagreed. The prevalence of Brazilian panelists' responses (40%) agreed with the definition, as opposed to 8% who disagreed. 8% were not sure. It appears that Brazilian panelists are more likely to associate intuition with feelings than their American counterpart. The majority of the responses (80%) (See Table 33) indicated that there was a consensus in the way of panelists agreeing that intuition is a feeling reiterating the prevalence of results from Round I (41%). Four percent were not sure.

Intuition is an instinct based on past experience. The major part of the American panelists (40%) agreed with the definition. 4% were not sure. The same percentage of Brazilian panelists (40%), also agreed with the definition in opposition of 8% who disagreed, and 8% who were not sure. The compound responses (80%) (Table 33) showed that panelists agree that intuition is an instinct and is based on past experience, confirming the percentage of responses on the theme *instinct* (41%); and the theme based on past experience (23%) from Round I. Twelve percent were not sure.

Intuition is an irrational, unconscious process. The prevailing percentage of American and Brazilian panelists' responses –36% and 44% respectively – disagreed with the definition of intuition as irrational and unconscious. 8% of American panelists and 12% of Brazilian agreed with the definition. The combined responses (84%) (Table 33) suggested that panelists disagreed that intuition is an irrational, unconscious process, restating results from Round I where the theme unconscious emerged only once.

Intuition is the direct, instantaneous, and integrated apprehension of truth. The preponderance of American panelists' responses (24%) agreed with the definition, and 40% of the Brazilian panelists concurred. Twenty percent of American panelists and 8% of Brazilian panelists disagreed. In this survey item, the preponderance of responses in the composite results (60%) (Table 33) implied that panelists agreed with the definition. There was a marked increased from the results from Round I for this theme (36%). Eight percent were not sure.

Intuition is a legitimate decision-making tool utilized by leaders in a myriad of business circumstances. Most American panelists (36%) agreed with the definition of intuition being a legitimate decision-making tool as opposed to 8% who disagreed. The major part of Brazilian panelists (44%) agreed with the statement, in opposition to 8% who disagreed; 4% were not sure. The bulk of panelists' responses (80%) (Table 33) pointed toward a consensual agreement with the definition. Four percent were not sure.

Intuition is a paranormal, irrational phenomenon. The negative responses from the American panelists comprised 44% of the whole group of panelists. The negative responses of the Brazilian panelists comprised 56%. In the mix results, the major part of American and Brazilian panelists (88%) (Table 33) disagreed with this statement. An increase of 3% that were in agreement with the statement was found, differing from the results from Round I in which the theme emerged only once, corresponding to 3% of the 33 participants.

Intuition is a rational, logical activity stemming from the realm of the inner wisdom. The preponderance of the American panelists agreed with the statement, corresponding to 40% while 4% did not agreed with statement. The Brazilian panelists' affirmative responses equaled 40%, contrasting with 8% who were in disagreement and 8% who were not sure. The majority of panelists' responses in the combined results (76%) (Table 33) agreed with the statement. Eight percent were not sure.

The role of intuition in my decision-making process can be best described as minimal. The majority of American panelists (40%) disagreed with this assertion, so did the majority of Brazilian panelists (40%). In opposition, 4% of American panelists indicated using intuition to a minimum in contrast to 16% of Brazilian panelists who stated using intuition to a minimum. The prevalence of panelists' aggregated responses (80%) disagreed with the statement confirming the findings from Round I where 18% stated that the use of intuition is minimal as opposed to 52% stating that the use of intuition was significant.

The role of intuition in my decision-making process can be best described as sporadic. The preponderance of the American panelists (28%) disagreed that the role of intuition in their decision-making is sporadic while 16% agreed with the assertion, as opposed to 32% of the Brazilian panelists who agreed to use intuition sporadically while 24% disagreed with the affirmation. In the compound results (see Table 33), the majority of panelists' responses (52%) disagreed with the statement confirming the findings from Round I where 30% responded that the use of intuition is sporadic against 52% indicating that the use of intuition was significant.

The role of intuition in my decision-making process can be best described as significant. The prevailing part of the American panelists' responses (28%) agreed to a significant role of intuition in their decision-making, whereas 12% indicated that the role of intuition is not significant. Similarly, the majority of Brazilian panelists (32%) agreed to a significant us of intuition in their decision-making while 28% disagreed with the statement. The mainstream of panelists' responses (56%) in the aggregated results (see Table 33), showed the highest percentage in the significant role of intuition, which corroborates the results from Round I where 52% panelists had classified their use of intuition in decision-making as significant.

I favor intuitive thinking in my decision-making process. The majority of American panelists (24%) indicated in their responses that they do not favor intuitive thinking in their decision-making, as opposed to 16% who agreed to favor intuitive thinking in their decision-making. Four percent were not sure. Representing a higher percentage, 36% of Brazilian panelists said that they favor intuitive thinking, and 16% said they do not favor intuitive thinking. Four percent were not sure. The prevalence of panelists' responses (48%) in the combined statistics of the two groups of panelists disagreed from the statement indicating that panelists did not favor intuition in decision-making. Such results deny the previous assertion that the use of intuition is significant. This survey item followed a logical flow from the preceding one in the way that it probed further in the panelists' preferences. The survey item that ensues was designed with the same purpose but responses further substantiated those of this survey item. Eight percent were not sure.

I favor logical and rational reasoning in my decision-making process. The most part of the American panelists (56%) indicated favoring rational and logical reasoning with 8% disagreeing with the affirmation. On the other hand, although the number of Brazilian panelists was higher than that of their American counterparts, the percentage of responses agreeing with this statement was lower (36%). The majority of panelists' responses (92%), shown in table 33, indicated that panelists favor logical and rational thinking in decision-making.

In my experience, I believe I reap benefits from using intuition in decision-making as opposed to traditional fact-based decision-making. The prevalence of American panelists (32%) disagreed that they reap benefits from using intuition in decision-making, in opposition to 12% who do believe they reap benefits from using intuition. The predominance of Brazilian panelists (36%) disagreed that they reap benefits from using intuition in decision-making, in opposition to 20% who do believe they reap benefits from using intuition. The combined results confirm these findings. Table 33 shows that panelists (56%) did not believe they reap benefits from the use of intuition, in contrast to 36%. Eight percent were not sure.

I rely on intuition in personnel-related business circumstances. In this survey item, the American panelists could not come to a consensus with 24% indicating not relying on intuition and 24% indicating not relying on intuition in personnel-related decisions. Conversely, 36% of the Brazilian panelists agreed that they rely on intuition in these circumstances, as opposed to 16% who stated they do not rely on intuition in personnel-related circumstances. The combined responses in agreement to this survey item (64%) present an opportunity for additional reflection on the three preceding survey items in the way that it may account for the panelists' generalization of their use of intuition in business decisions as significant.

I rely on intuition in strategic decision-making circumstances. The main part of the American panelists' responses (24%) was in disagreement with this statement suggesting that they do not rely on intuition in strategic decisions. On the other hand, 20% of the same group agreed that they rely on intuition for strategic purposes. The Brazilian contingent, on the other hand, predominantly (36%) indicated relying on intuition for strategic reasons, whereas 16% indicated not relying on intuition with that intent. The compound results shows, in this survey item, that 52% of the panelists disagreed with the statement indicating that intuition is not very much relied upon in strategic decisions. Conversely, the majority of responses in Round I (41%) indicated the use of intuition as significant. The minority of responses (48%) indicated reliance on intuition in strategic decisions.

I rely on intuition to determine business performance gaps. Similar results were found in the American panelists' responses to this item with 24% indicating not relying on intuition to determine performance gaps, and 20% indicating relying on intuition for those purposes. A higher percentage of responses were found in the Brazilian group (28%) who indicated that they rely on intuition to determine performance gaps. However, 28% of the same group also indicated not relying on intuition for that purpose, suggesting that the group could not come to a consensus. In this survey item, the aggregated percentage (20%) of the panelists indicated relying on intuition as opposed to 76% of the total panelists who indicated that they do not rely on intuition to determine business performance gaps (Table 33).

I rely on intuition when assessing market, economic and political scenarios. The majority of the American panelist's responses (36%) showed that they do not rely on intuition to assess market, economic and political scenarios. Only 4% stated using intuition for those reasons. Correspondingly, 36% of the Brazilian panelists also attested not relying on intuition for those purposes, but 16% agreed that they rely on intuition when making those assessments. Eight percent were not sure. The major part of the combined responses stated that 64% panelists do not rely on intuition to assess market, economic and political scenarios, whereas 32% rely on intuition when making these decisions (Table 33). Four percent were not sure.

Intuition strongly impacts my decision-making on cost reduction and performance improvement. In 28% of the American panelists' responses, it was found that this group does not believe intuition strongly affects decision-making on cost reduction and performance improvement, with 12% indicating that intuition strongly influences decision-making on cost reduction and performance improvement. Similarly, a higher percentage of Brazilian panelists (36%) indicated that intuition does not affect decision-making on cost reduction and performance improvement, with 16% indicating that they perceive as strong the impact of intuition on cost reduction and performance improvement decisions. The aggregated percentages for the two groups of panelists (68% of the responses) suggested that panelists do not rely on intuition in those circumstances, in opposition to 32% of panelists who do. In opposition, the majority of responses in Round I (41%) indicated the use of intuition as significant.

Given the new levels of complexity in decision-making, there is a growing interrelationship between intuition and logical reasoning in decision-making. The majority of the American panelists' responses (36%) agreed with the statement, with 4% disagreeing and 4% not being sure. The major part of the Brazilian panelists (52%) also agreed with the statement as opposed to 4% who were in disagreement. The compound results (88%) (Table 33) indicated to agree with the growing relationship between intuition and logical decision-making. Four percent were not sure.

Corporations ought to encourage the formal development intuitive thinking to enhance decision-making. The majority of responses from the American group of panelists (24%) were in agreement with the suggestion, whereas 12% disagreed and 8% was not sure. The major part of responses from the Brazilian group of panelists (32%) were in favor of corporations encouraging the formal development of intuition, as opposed to 20% who were not in favor, and 4% were not sure. The preponderance of responses in the aggregated results (56%) agreed with the statement, as opposed to 32%. 12% were not sure.

Table 34 describes the combined statistical survey results of American and Brazilian panelists' responses.

Table 34

Combined Survey Results

Survey Indicators/Aggregated Percentages			
Survey Items	Not Sure	Disagree	Agree
1. Intuition is a feeling.	4%	16%	80%
2. Intuition is an instinct based on past experience.	12%	8%	80%
3. Intuition is an irrational, unconscious process.	0%	84%	16%
4. Intuition is the direct, instantaneous and integrated apprehension of truth.	8%	32%	60%

Survey Items	Not Sure	Disagree	Agree
5. Intuition is a legitimate decision-making tool utilized by leaders in a myriad of business circumstances.	4%	16%	80%
6. Intuition is a paranormal, irrational phenomenon.	0%	88%	12%
7. Intuition is a rational, logical activity stemming from the realm of the inner wisdom.	8%	16%	76%
8. The role of intuition in my decision-making process can be best described as minimal.	0%	80%	20%
9. The role of intuition in my decision-making process can be best described as sporadic.	0%	52%	48%
10. The role of intuition in my decision-making process can be best described as significant.	0%	44%	56%
11. I favor intuitive thinking in my decision-making process.	8%	48%	44%
12. I favor logical and rational reasoning in my decision-making process.	0%	8%	92%
13. In my experience I believe I reap benefits from using intuition in decision-making as opposed to			
traditional fact-based decision-making.	8%	56%	36%
14. I rely on intuition in personnel-related business circumstances.	0%	36%	64%
15. I rely on intuition in strategic decision-making circumstances.	0%	52%	48%
16. I rely on intuition to determine business performance gaps.	4%	76%	20%
17. I rely on intuition when assessing market, economic and political scenarios.	4%	64%	32%

Survey Items	Not Sure	Disagree	Agree
18. Intuition strongly impacts my decision-making on cost reduction and performance improvement.	8%	68%	32%
19. Given the new levels of complexity in decision- making, and the discoveries of the magnitude of the human cognition, there is a growing inter-relationship between intuition and logical reasoning in decision-making.	4%	8%	88%
20. Corporations ought to encourage the formal the formal development of intuitive thinking to enhance decision-making.	12%	32%	56%

Computing the frequency distribution per survey item provides a deeper understanding of the responses. The distribution of the responses to the survey questions revealed a value for standard deviation of approximately 1 spreading across the range from *unsure* to *strongly agree* or 4+/-1; a measure of how widely spread the values in the resulting data are. The average answer or the extreme value for survey items 1, 2, 5, 12, and 19 was 4, which corresponds to *agree,* indicating that the majority of responses for those survey items were clustered around the survey indicators *agree and strongly agree.* Therefore, the majority of the panelists agreed that intuition is a feeling, and an instinct. Panelists also agreed that although intuition is a legitimate decision-making tool (mean value of 4); they favor rational, logical reasoning when making decisions (mean value of 4.04). However, the majority of panelists concurred that there is a growing interrelationship between intuition and rational decision-making. Table 35 depicts the itemized means and standard deviations of the responses of the 25 American and Brazilian panelists who responded to the 20 Likert-type scale survey items.

Table 35

Means and Standard Deviations for Survey Items in Round II

Survey Items	Mean	Standard Deviation
1. Intuition is a feeling.	4.04	1.03
2. Intuition is an instinct based on past experience.	4.00	0.80
3. Intuition is an irrational, unconscious process.	2.04	0.90
4. Intuition is the direct, instantaneous and integrated apprehension of truth.	3.28	1.24
5. Intuition is a legitimate decision-making tool utilized by leaders in a myriad of business circumstances.	4.00	1.01
6. Intuition is a paranormal, irrational phenomenon.	1.88	1.14
7. Intuition is a rational, logical activity stemming from the realm of the inner wisdom.	3.72	0.87
8. The role of intuition in my decision-making process can be best described as minimal.	2.20	1.09
9. The role of intuition in my decision-making process can be best described as sporadic.	3.00	1.26
10. The role of intuition in my decision-making process can be best described as significant.	3.16	1.55
11. I favor intuitive thinking in my decision-making process.	3.00	1.13
12. I favor logical and rational reasoning in my decision-making process.	4.04	0.72
13. In my experience I believe I reap benefits from using intuition in decision-making as opposed to traditional fact-based decision-making.	2.88	1.07
14. I rely on intuition in personnel-related business circumstances.	3.36	1.05
15. I rely on intuition in strategic decision-making circumstances.	3.04	1.11
16. I rely on intuition to determine business performance gaps.	2.44	0.94
17. I rely on intuition when assessing market, economic and political scenarios.	2.68	1.04
18. Intuition strongly impacts my decision-making on cost reduction and performance improvement.	2.60	1.09
19. Given the new levels of complexity in decision- making, and the discoveries of the magnitude of the human cognition, there is a growing inter-relationship between intuition and logical reasoning in decision-making.	4.00	0.74
20. Corporations ought to encourage the formal the formal development of intuitive thinking to enhance decision-making.	3.48	1.17
Total	3.14	1.23

All values of means and standard deviations for the responses to the survey items are illustrated in Figure 5. A standard scale of 20 was used as the value axis (Y). The category axis (X) depicts the survey items. The graphic shows the values for each of the survey indicators, which when combined, yielded the percentages in Table 33. The highest values were again for survey items 1, 2,3,5,6,8,12, and 19 meaning that panelists achieved the highest consensus on these survey items. The value 18 for survey item 12 represents that there was an almost complete consensus. The highest value was 18 for survey items 12, *I favor logical and rational reasoning in my decision-making;* 16, *I rely on intuition to determine business performance gaps,* and 19 respectively.

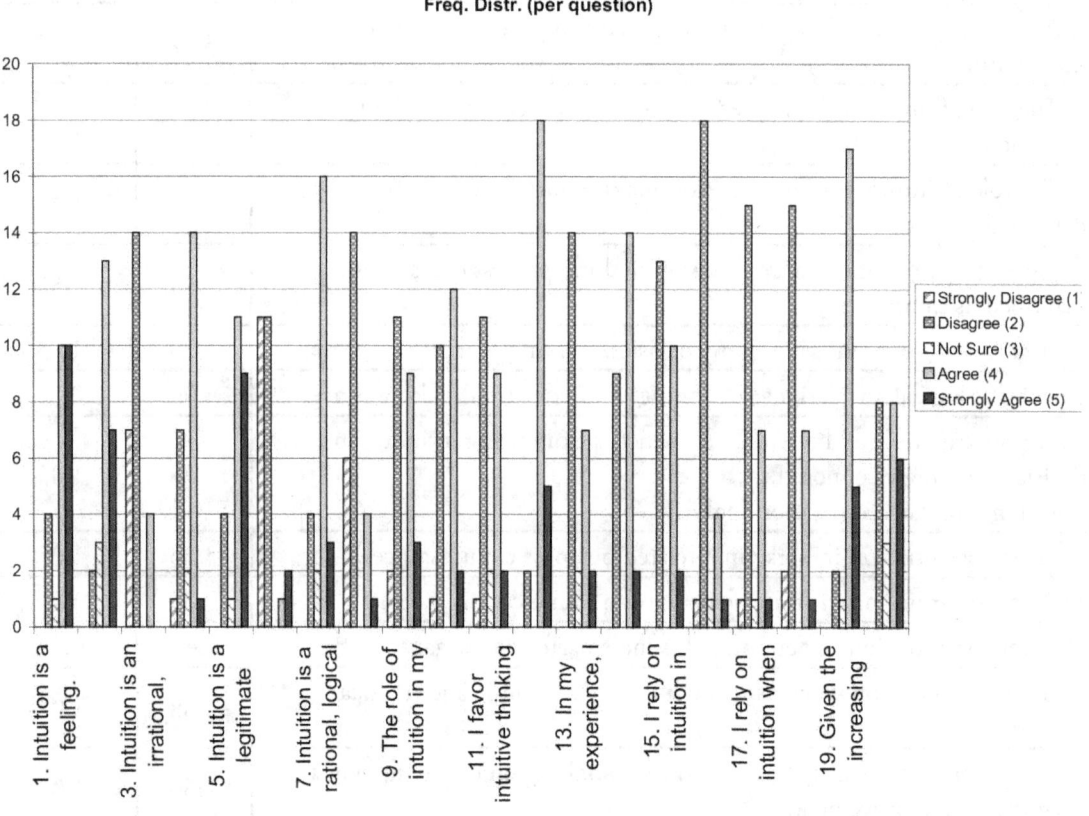

Figure 5. Frequency distribution per question.

Figure 6 depicts the total frequency distribution of responses to the Likert-type scale survey in Round II per survey indicator. The value for survey indicator *agree* is 195. The value for survey indicator *disagree* is 188.

Freq. Dist. (total)

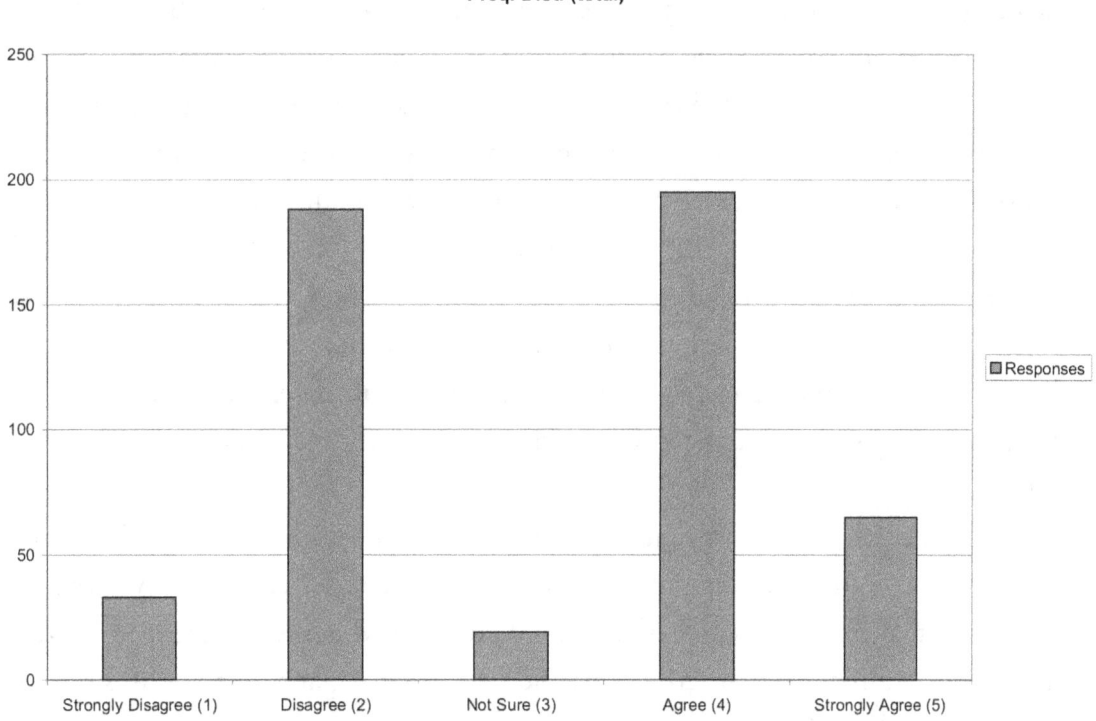

Figure 6. Total frequency distribution per survey indicator.

Summary of Findings

Three central issues were explored in the study: the definition of intuition, the role of intuition in business decision-making, and the role of intuition in strategy formulation, cost reduction and performance improvement decision-making. Regarding the definition of intuition, American and Brazilian bank leaders consensually agreed that the definitions of intuition being simultaneously a feeling, and an instinct based on past experiences. American and Brazilian bank leaders also agreed that intuition is not an irrational and unconscious process. Both factions also assented that intuition is a rational activity stemming from the realm of the inner wisdom. Additionally, both groups consented that intuition is a legitimate decision-making tool utilized by leaders in a myriad of decisions. Conversely, American and Brazilian bank leaders favor rational and logical reasoning process when making business decisions. Concerning the role intuition plays on daily business decision-making, both groups consensually disagreed that it plays a minimal role. Nonetheless, the percentage of Brazilian bank leaders who stated that it plays a minimal role was substantially higher (see table 32). The preponderance of American and Brazilian panelists agreed that it is significant (see Table 32). A slightly higher number of Brazilian bankers reported that the role of intuition in their decision-making is significant.

Opinion was polarized regarding the percentage of American and Brazilian panelists who considered the role of intuition as sporadic (see Table 32). A higher number of Brazilian bankers chose that option (see table 32). However, collectively, the percentage of American and Brazilian panelists who stated that the role of intuition in their decision-making was significant was nearly evenly distributed. The percentage of American bank leaders who favor rational and fact-based means of decision-making was significantly higher as opposed to their Brazilian counterparts. The percentages combined for both groups indicated a consensual preference for rational and logical reasoning when making decisions. Both groups indicated that they do not reap benefits from intuition in decision-making. The Brazilian contingent reported to rely on intuition for personnel-related reasons as well as for strategic purposes. The American counterparts could not reach a consensus on both accounts.

While American bank leaders reported not relying on intuition when making strategy formulations, an equal percentage of Brazilian bank leaders stated that they do rely on intuition when making those kinds of decisions. Areas in which American and Brazilian bank leaders agreed include cost reductions and performance gaps. Both groups reported that they do not rely on intuition in those determinations. American and Brazilian bank leaders indicated that they do not rely on intuition when making market, economic and political assessments. Further, both American and Brazilian bank leaders concurred that there is a growing interrelationship between intuition and logical reasoning, and that corporations ought to develop intuition in their employees. The fact that Brazilian group had a higher percentage in each of the responses can be attributed to a higher number of panelists from that nationality in Round II. Consequently, reasons of a cultural nature can be attributed to the difference in the percentages.

Conclusions

In keeping with the purpose of this Delphi study, it was noted that American and Brazilian bank leaders agree on the three main research questions, namely the definitions of intuition, its use and growing interrelationship, and the need for its development in the banking industry. Any explicit divergences or convergences of opinion became diffused and as such, were difficult to determine as a function of the following three factors: (a) the uneven number of American and Brazilian panelists in the second round; and (b) the inability to reach a consensus on some of the Likert-type scale survey items; and (c) seemingly contradictory responses to the use of intuition in daily decision-making and for strategic purposes, cost reduction and performance gaps.

Although these results do not necessarily mean that panelists do not favor intuition, the almost perfect unanimity of American and Brazilian panelists' indications of the significant role of intuition in their decision-making and the subsequent indication of the low use and impact of intuition in strategic, cost reduction and performance gaps seems to revoke and invalidate the assertion that the use of intuition is significant in Round I and in the survey. Even though there was no reported or perceptible reason for the contradiction in panelists' responses, the issue of the use of intuition being deemed as significant as indicated by the majority of responses in Round I might suggest a possible error in the interpretation of the questions and survey items. From a different perspective, the contradiction or ambiguity in the responses might be an indication of the ability of American and Brazilian bank leaders to deal with ambivalence when faced by uncertainty, while being capable of adapting their responses according to the situation.

Despite the fact that neurophysiologic research has elucidated the difference between intuition and instinct, subjugating the latter to the sphere of the reptilian brain that programs human beings for survival and reproduction (Rapaille, 2006), the responses seem to indicate a protracted confusion surrounding the two terms. The responses from the American and the Brazilian groups of bank leaders confirmed Rowan's (1989) Goleman's (1998), and Cooper and Sawaf's (1997) contention that in the business circles leaders refer to the term intuition as insight, hunch or gut feeling in contrast to other contemporary meanings that equate intuition to the inner voice (Familoni, 2002); a direct grasping of the truth (Yogananda, 2003); and Mintzberg's (1994) assertion that strategy is synthesis, later corroborated by Garmston's (2006) definition of intuitive thinking as macro thinking. In a similar study, Schmidt (1995) had appropriately remarked that the Western society neither promotes the reflective and receptive mind-set essential to decision-making in an expand consciousness nor does it support efforts to integrate information with the inherent knowledge.

Regarding the aspects above, the findings from this study did not diverge from the expectations or from commonly established and time-honored perceptions of the topic of intuition in the banking industry. Nonetheless, the fact that American and Brazilian panelists alike agreed that more effective and creative decision-making calls for the development of intuition in corporations, may be an indication that the intuitive ability may just represent the missing factor.

Summary

Chapter 4 reviewed the procedures adopted in the computerized version of the Delphi method across two rounds of data collection from a panel of American and Brazilian banking leaders. A web-based professional survey site called Zoomerang.com, to which the expert panelists were given access, hosted the two rounds, the first one qualitative and the second one quantitative. The preponderance of opinions was achieved in the two rounds of the Delphi thus consigning Round III to the presentation of results to the panelists. The high pressure coupled with the itinerant nature of the panelists' jobs was a deterrent in retaining the level of panelists' participation throughout the study.

Analysis of data obtained on Round I and Round II was presented in narrative and statistical forms with tables and graphic representations illustrating the data results for the two rounds. Interpretation of the similarities, comparisons, and disparities was discussed thus setting the stage for a deeper reflection on the research findings and recommendations in chapter 5.

Even though the findings of this research indicate that factual and numerical data rest at the core of financial decisions and therefore drive most of these decisions for American and Brazilian bankers, the predominance of panelists agreed on the use and importance of intuition in decision-making. In the quantitative phase of this Delphi study, panelists further concurred on the growing interrelationship between intuition and rational decision-making.

CHAPTER 5: CONCLUSIONS, IMPLICATIONS, AND RECOMMENDATIONS

The general problem was that decision makers in the banking industry face numerous constraints posed by increasing uncertainties in the realm of global geopolitical disparities in resultant financial analysis and forecast. Partial financial data further aggravates decision-making. The specific problem was that conventional analytical processes that remain unquestioned in corporations preclude the integration of intuition as an innovative and legitimate decision-making tool. Consequently, protracted analytical methods thwart expeditious and effective decision-making processes. The intent of this Delphi study was to investigate the ways in which American and Brazilian bank leaders perceive and define intuition and the extent to which intuition is used in daily business decision-making. Chapter 4 portrayed the responses from the panel of experts to the qualitative and quantitative rounds of this Delphi study. Chapter 5 addresses the research problem in light of the results gathered *and is organized by the following six topics: (a) limitations of the research study, (b)* validity and reliability, *(c)* ethical dimensions, (d) conclusions, (e) recommendations, and (f) summary.

Limitations

Chapter 1 discussed the limitations that restricted this research study. Such demarcations included the panelists' traits, the nature of the instruments, restrictions to the generalizability of the results, researcher's bias, external validity, attrition, and the characteristics of the Delphi method. This research study was restricted to executives of two different nationalities from a broad spectrum of positions in the banking industry. The generalizability of the results of this study may have been compromised by five factors. The first one regards the validity of the open-ended questions to Round I. At the on-set of Round I a pilot test of the open-ended questions was undertaken and an invitation was extended to panelists with view to obtain their comments, opinions, and critiques regarding the choice of words and clarity of the questions. Notwithstanding those efforts, no comments were received precluding any opportunity to review the questions. Instead, panelists unanimously opted for responding directly to the questions. It is speculated that this can be attributable to the panelists' scarcity of time. However, that deficiency was later reflected in some panelists' responses to question three. Some panelists seemed to have interpreted question two as similar or identical to question three by way of their responses, even though the latter required an elaboration to the former. Had some form of preliminary review been made, the clarity of the questions could have been improved and the level of understanding could have been higher. The occurrence underscores the importance of a pilot study.

The second limiting factor of the validity of the research study refers to a hiatus in the demographic data collected from panelists. No questions related to the panelists' personal interest or involvement in the subject of intuition were asked. Such kind of information, if incorporated into the demographic questionnaire, could have been useful in two ways: (a) establishing correlations between those panelists whose higher use of and reliance on intuition in their decision-making result from self-directed endeavors; and (b) elucidating panelists' perceptions, views, opinions, and thoughts about the role of intuition in business decision-making.

The third limiting factor concerned a disadvantage inherent to the cross-sectional research strategy in that it "limits the comparability of groups" (Salkind, 2003, p.196). Although bank leaders from other nationalities may share the same views, this study is restricted to the comparison between the two nationalities of the panelists. An offshoot of this shortcoming was the number of withdrawals prior to and during the study. Albeit the duration of the study was minimized (Salkind, 2003), the number of withdrawals was significant.

Another shortcoming involved the qualitative aspect of the study. The number of non-respondents had an undeniable effect on the findings which would have differed had the entire population been considered (Salkind, 2003). A considerable amount of time was devoted to attempting, by phone and by email, to motivate non-respondents to join the study again and offer their contribution. Ultimately, respect for the rule of voluntary participation prevailed. Finally, although adequate measures and cautions were undertaken to ensure compliance with the ethical policies of sampling, methodological, and report of research findings, the lack of sufficient training in designing and conducting a "legitimate survey" (Neuman, 1997, p.265) was a determining factor in any errors that may have arisen.

One final consideration is that Neuman (1997) stressed the importance of having "an awareness of the time dimension" (p.28) when conducting research "because different research questions or issues incorporate time in different ways" (p.28). The time dimension was not an anticipated aspect in this study and represented a limiting factor escaping the management of this Delphi study. Such constraint pertained to the period of its inception – December 2006 through January 2007. This coincided with the season holiday worldwide and summer vacation in the Southern hemisphere. At that time, most panelists were away and unavailable to participate in the study. The occurrence caused a three-week delay in receiving responses. Although the interruption did not deter panelists from participating in Round I and did not impinge on the quality of responses, it encumbered the panelists' intense workload, subsequently leading to attrition in Round II.

Ethical Dimensions

Considerations of an ethical nature circumscribed three aspects of this Delphi study: (a) the population sample; (b) the instruments of data collection; and (c) the researcher's bias. This research study explored the differences of opinions and perceptions of two distinct groups of 33 bank leaders. Sampling of the panelists adhered to the strictest parameters of face validity (Neuman, 1997) and choice of 20 participants as the optimum number for homogeneous groups (Jeffery, Ley, Bennun & McLaren, 2000). Regarding the former, panelists who participated in this study met the requirement of being banking experts. Concerning the latter, a sample population of 33 exceeds the optimal number.

Further ethical implications include observance to the Collaborative IRB Training Initiative (CITI) (2006). Both groups received equal and respectful treatment in the way of being duly educated as to the nature and requirements of the study, being allowed the freedom to withdraw from the study without penalty, not being submitted to any psychological and physical pressure or constraints; and having their anonymity and confidentiality of responses preserved. Communications with the panelists were conducted initially in the panelist's native language–either English or Portuguese. However, panelists in this study are bilingual and felt more comfortable communicating in English, the *lingua franca* of the study.

Attempts were made to address the ethical issue of congruity by means of a plan to conduct a pilot test of the Web-based data collection software and Zoomerang.com survey site and of the open-ended questions to Round I with view to measure internal validity. Nonetheless, as previously stated, the panelists were not forthcoming in providing comments and suggestions to the open-ended questions. There are two possible interpretations for the occurrence. The first one could be a function of the time constraints under which the panelists operate daily. The second one might be construed as the questions meeting all requirements of congruity and reliability. Although, the former seems to be a more likely possibility, no panelists refrained from responding to the questions.

An additional ethical issue implicates the deliberation of the most appropriate time to cease data collection to ensure that all areas of the research were covered. Data collection ceased at the end of Round II after panelists had stopped visiting the survey Website. At that stage of the study, 25 panelists had responded––a number superior to the minimum required for consensus. Additionally, several reminders had been made over the telephone and sent via email for nearly two weeks. A few panelists were traveling and would only be available at the end of the month. It is arguable whether further wait would have increased participation.

Another ethical consideration concerns the partially arbitrary design of the survey ordinal scale. As a defense, it must be pointed out that although subjective to an extent, scale options were drawn from Creswell's (2000) examples of ordinal scales. Further, other ethical issues that are likely to emerge in research studies (Creswell, 2000) regard respect for the honest and complete report of research findings with its limitations, unexpected disruptions, and decisions to disregard responses. These were observed in this study and the combined results of the two methods of data collection were submitted to the mentor and committee members as a provisional external audit.

Conclusions

Considering that, the intrinsic design of this study aimed at reaching a consensus regarding the use of intuition in financial decision-making in the banking environment, and sought to predict future trends in the use of intuition in decision-making, this Delphi study presented the most appropriate methodology for collecting data. "Delphi is a dynamic methodology which was especially suitable for studying topics with ill-defined boundaries" (Schmidt, 1995, p. 222). An additional benefit of this Delphi method included the opportunity for a broad spectrum of experts to participate in the study without being constrained by geography, or expenditures (Schmidt, 1995). Moreover, the Delphi provided a forum where bank experts could offer their views confident in the protection of their confidentiality. In particular, the Delphi, as an educational, self-reflective instrument, and as "a future's methodology" (p.222) engaged the bank panelists in a learning process that opened the prospects of future leadership.

Not all the 33 panelists who participated in this study completed the three rounds. Twenty-five completed the second round of data collection. This is not a surprising statistic given that high dropout rates constitute a deficiency in Delphi studies (Schmidt). On the other hand, this may be suggestive of bank leaders' degree of current and future commitment to the topic of intuition in the sphere of financial decisions.

The tenets of the problem statement were that despite evidence of the limitations of factual data to support decisions and the need for innovative decision-making approaches, partiality and predilection for conventional factual and numerical data in the banking industry are still determining factors in financial decisions. The bank experts' responses corroborated these theories. Bank experts' emotional and instinctual characterization of intuition may be the underlying reason for the preference. The Western philosophical and scientific conditioning that conceals intuitive abilities underneath layers of "fear of regressing into some primitive anthropomorphic grip" (p. 232) seems to prevail. Such a perspective prevents bank leaders from utilizing intuition in strategic, cost reduction and performance related decisions. The findings of Khatri & Ng's (2000) investigations and the findings of this study converge in verifying that intuition is used to a lesser extent in the banking industry

In keeping with the exploratory attribute of qualitative studies, the questions and survey items in this Delphi study were designed to gradually and increasingly disclose and unveil layers of perceptions and decision-making patterns. Therefore, supported by the questions that framed this study, the findings of this study can be summarized and assembled into the following main streams:

Frame questions: How do American and Brazilian bank leaders define intuition? What are American and Brazilian bank leaders' views, beliefs, and attitudes regarding the nature of intuition? In response to these frame questions, bank leaders' responses were consistent on both rounds. Panelists believe intuition is a feeling and an instinct that result from previous experiences. Additionally, panelists agreed on the points that intuition is not opposed to a rational activity. Although the panelists' views were not spontaneously offered but rather, they reacted to a proposed definition of intuition as being a rational activity that can be accessed from the realm of the inner wisdom. In the recognition of a truthful statement, panelists' consensus was that intuition connects one with a direct knowing and an internal reservoir of wisdom. The panelists' support to the notion that intuition is a legitimate decision-making tool utilized by leaders in a myriad of circumstances suggests two thoughts: (a) that they acknowledge the use of intuition in decisions in the banking environment in addition to the traditional numerical data; and (b) they recognize that intuition is a rightful, and genuine reference system for sound decision-making.

Frame question: What benefits do American and Brazilian bank leaders gain from using intuition in decision-making as opposed to traditional fact-based decision-making? Bank leaders affirmed that they reap little or no benefit from using intuition in their financial decisions. Once again, this affirmation conflicts with the panelists' alleged significant use of intuition.

Frame question: How do American and Brazilian bank leaders describe their decision-making process? In which decision-making business circumstances do American and Brazilian bank leaders prefer to rely on intuition? When questioned about the role of intuition in daily business decisions bank leaders affirmed that their use of intuitive thinking in generic business decision-making is significant. Conversely, when questioned about the role of intuition in specific financial decisions involving strategic planning, cost reduction and performance improvements, panelists' responses descended from significant to minimal. When the panelists indicated that the role of intuition is significant in their daily business decision-making and later advocated a preference for logical and rational decision-making in financial decisions, they seemed to be contradicting themselves. There appears to be an incongruity among bank experts' perceived role and benefits of intuition in decision-making and their preferred decision-making tools.

Frame question: What are the American and Brazilian bank leaders' experiences of the impact of intuition on decision-making involving strategic formulation, cost reduction and performance gaps and improvement? Bank leaders' agreed that their use of intuition in decisions involving strategy formulation, cost reduction and performance gaps and improvement, and assessing market and political scenarios is minimal. Panelists also consensually agreed that they reap little benefit from intuitively guided financial decisions.

Frame question: What are the American and Brazilian bank leaders' perceptions of the interrelationship between intuition and decision-making? Bank leaders were in accord that there is a growing relationship between intuition and logical and rational decision-making. Here the inconsistency with the preference for rational and fact-based means of reaching decisions was further accentuated by the bank experts' acknowledgement that intuition and logical reasoning are complementary when compared to the affirmation that they favor logical reasoning when making decisions. By accepting the harmonization between the two polarities, the bank panelists can foresee the increasing prospect of intuition and rational thought as integral parts of a balanced and "creative union between the outer and the inner" (Schmidt, 1995, p. 227). In lieu of an alternative path, there is the prospect of making decisions that "transcends the differences and lifts our awareness into a higher order of complexity" (227).

Frame question: What are the views of American and Brazilian bank leaders regarding the development of intuition in banking corporations? Bank leaders believe that it behooves corporations to find ways to explore and develop the creative power of intuitive abilities in their employees for enhanced decision-making. These views are in agreement with

Familoni (2002) who put forward that the development of intuitive capabilities can effect changes in the evolution of leadership paradigms.

Considering that no significant difference in the responses of American and Brazilian panelists was observed, it is unavoidable to ponder on the possible similarities between the two groups. Two factors may serve as plausible explanations: (a) Panelists in the two groups work for American banks. The cultural influence of the American culture is pervasive in our society and in the corporate world; and (b) the two nationalities share common Western origins, which could account for the panelists' preference for the rational approach. The question remains if different samplings from Eastern cultures would lead to different results.

It is recognized that the results could be attributable to factors such as sampling, instrument, or time limitations. Therefore, the findings of the study are inconclusive. Although further research would be needed, this study accomplished its exploratory and investigative task.

Implications

Notwithstanding the fact that the questions framing this study were specific in nature and focused on the banking industry, the findings may not be relevant, pertinent, valid or applicable to all banking areas of specialization. Given that the focal points of this study rested on the definition of intuition, its interconnection with rational thought, and the bank leaders' decision-making style, they will serve as the underpinnings for the discussion on the implications of this study.

The most noteworthy inference that may be made from the results of this Delphi study relates to the responses to the open-ended question 1, the statistical results to survey item 12, 19 and survey item 20 respectively given that the panelists achieved the highest level of consensus on those questions and survey items. In the first instance, the majority of responses equated intuition with feelings and instincts. In the second instance, panelists showed a propensity to agree with the statement *given the increasing level of complexities in decision-making, there is a growing interrelationship between intuitive and rational thinking in decision-making.* On survey item 20, panelists also agreed that *corporations* ought *to develop intuition towards enhanced decision-making.* Conversely, on survey item 12 with the statement *I favor logical and rational reasoning in my decision-making* a nearly perfect consensus and unanimity were achieved, representing 92% of the responses.

The disparity between the two opposing results may imply three possibilities. First, albeit banking panelists accept the value of intuition as a legitimate decision-making tool, they have a penchant to associate their decision-making styles with a more logical and rational approach. Second, since a third round was not performed, no efforts were made to probe and further investigate and ascertain whether the panelists' attitudes are guided by personal or professional preference, or by extraneous reasons. This is admittedly, a limitation of this study. Therefore, it can only be speculated that the preference of bankers in the banking job functions in this study may not apply across the board to other bank job functions.

Evidence of this assertion is the example of hedge funds professionals. In hedge funds operations, timing is of the essence. Contrary to traditional decision-making strategies, hedge funds experts utilize extreme advantages, resorting to unorthodox decision-making tools, which afford a faster and more globalized perspective of possible outcomes (Peter Weil, February 10, 2007, interview). Weil's views are confirmed by Gaspar and Napolitano (2007) who stated that there is an intangible aspect characterizing hedge funds professionals, which some call intuition and which is frequently associated with the manner in which such managers and leaders make decisions. Based on these considerations, the indication, as per the findings in this study, that the banking panelists' use of intuition is significant may be expressive of an increasing realization of the importance and effectiveness of intuitive thinking to achieve results with a maximum speed and accuracy.

Implications to Leadership

Vision, as a fundamental factor that differentiates leadership from management, is a perceived synthesis of the whole enabled by intuition. The projection of an ideal, an aspiration, a target into the future, more often than not, precludes the knowledge of verifiable information. It is this fusion of intuitive elements in the psyche that creates the blueprint of manifested realities. Herein lay one of the most profound implications of this study to the exercise of leadership.

Evidenced by the contradictions in the panelists' responses, it appears that it is difficult for American and Brazilian bank leaders to determine, with any degree of precision, the extent to which intuition is used in general business and specific financial decisions. Further, it appears to be challenging to American and Brazilian bank leaders to admit the use decision-making tools other than numerical data given that both careers and massive sums of money are at stake. While privately commenting on the results for Round II, one panelist rationalized that bank leaders customarily seek to provide a consistent rational explanation for financial decisions since leaders often confront the need to defend and substantiate financial decisions. Hence, the tendency to base decisions on factual experience as opposed to intuition, notwithstanding leaders may privately acknowledge that intuition plays a prominent role (see appendix M). The panelist in question did not provide any reasons for the inability to justify and defend the use of intuitive thinking. This behavior could be attributed to an enduring perception of intuition as belonging in the realm of the emotions and instincts, which has been stereotyped as essentially a female characteristic (Rogers and Wiseman (2005/2006) and thus has no place in the financial environment.

It is fitting to quote Schmidt (1995) in her analysis of panel responses in similar Delphi study, in which she posited that it is understandable that:

> Members of the panel would be cautious in their predictions of such an immense shift in the way we orient ourselves to our world. After all, we do live in a world where we are encouraged to seek wisdom and encouragement outside ourselves (p.220).

On the other hand, the duality in the responses may indicate that bank leaders have the ability to deal with ambivalence when faced by uncertainty, while being capable of adapting their responses according to the situation. The fact remains that decisions continue to be made with partial and sometimes biased information. One way of closing the information gaps would be by incorporating intuition in decision-making. Nonetheless, bank leaders' current understanding of intuition as belonging in the realm of the emotions and instincts may be a deterrent to the utilization of more encompassing and innovative decision-making techniques and tools in a financial environment.

The panelists' consensual responses to the affirmations that intuition is a rational brain activity stemming from the sphere of inner wisdom and is a legitimate decision-making tool may reflect two possibilities: Firstly, bank leaders' agreement with the two statements, amplified the panelists' initial lay classification of intuition, acknowledging them as truthful. Secondly, intuition is a complex, multi-faceted issue of difficult definition (Rogers and Wiseman, 2005/2006).

As an additional data that emerged from the research, the unanimous agreement that organizations require an incentive to the development of intuition for improved decision-making further corroborates bank leaders' acknowledgement of intuition as a valid decision-making tool, either as a central factor or as a supplement. The repercussions of these findings to leadership and to the industry as a whole indicate that bank leaders operate under the grip of limited decision-making tools. Under the stimulus of corporate developmental initiatives, a new and broader understanding of intuition can begin to develop past earlier historical conditionings and start being used as an innovative and wide-ranging decision-making tool. Table 36 summarizes the findings for the research questions in this study.

Table 36

Significance to Leadership

Research Question	Results	Significance to Leadership
Definition of Intuition	Intuition is an instinctual feeling and stems from past experiences	Perceptions may prevent bank leaders from incorporating the use of intuition
Role of Intuition in Decision-Making	Significant in generic or personnel decisions	Bank leaders associate intuition with emotions (Rogers and Wiseman, 2005/2006)
Role of Intuition in Decision Making Related to Cost Reduction and Performance Gaps	Reported as significant but the rational, factual approach to financial decision-making is still favored	Contradiction in the responses evidence panelists' difficulty in determining and admitting the use of intuition
Development of Intuition in Organizations	Escalating global volatility and restricted information will require leaders to rethink decision-making	Organizations should incorporate intuition in leadership development for enhanced decision-making

Predictions from Delphi

Throughout history, the Delphi oracle enjoyed a worldwide reputation for its accurate predictive capabilities. Named after the oracle, the Delphi method is used for scientific prognostic purposes. From an extrapolative perspective, if the panelists' responses represent a movement, a shift in consciousness, then the findings of this study can have significant implications to the current perceptions and purposes of leadership, the way leaders perceive and confront global crises, and how they develop associates. The forecast scenario would be an evolutionary step towards harnessing, nurturing, and expanding the full potential of individual mental, psychological, and spiritual resources, reconciling intuition with rational thought, and transcending the limitations and impermanence of reasoning based on facts. Schmidt (1995) hit a nerve by urging that leaders open up to an intuitive and transcendental dimension of leadership that coexists with the secular. According to Schmidt, the role of leaders is not to organize resources for changes in structures, to move from crises through crises, but to act as facilitators in the evolution of consciousness of collaborators. Dealing with crises with limited options is a circular motion; it means having more of the same changes. "Often changes is simply rearrangement of what already is or it is simply movement on a continuum between poles" (p. 223). Going past changes embracing the polarities of reason and intuition toward breakthroughs is an evolutionary forward movement. This is future in the making. Nevertheless, "change can only be effected from within through a process of self-reflection" (p.223). Only leaders who can achieve that kind of inner change are fit to inspire it in others through training or education, but, most importantly, by example.

Akin to the Delphi oracle, the predictive beauty of the Delphi method lies in guiding the panel experts through a process of remembering, that which is already known within. In doing so, the Delphi educates panelists on how to access that inner knowing and turn the future into the present. Change that is driven by introspection increases future possibilities. In this regard, this Delphi study may serve as a humble contribution.

As a resonance of the problem statement, the predictions of this Delphi study are that the complexities of the financial market and the world at large will continue to increase, and the outcomes will remain even less predictable. Bank leaders worldwide are part of the integrated whole; and therefore, as decision-makers, are part of the problem. By considering innovative decision-making tools, such as intuition, bank leaders might be better equipped to deal with current and future challenges. Such an evolution might affect our current perceptions of leadership decision-making processes and the way leaders deal with crises.

Future Research

Supplementary studies with larger population samples involving the banking industry, and utilizing the same nationalities could be useful and beneficial toward higher comparability of the same groups (Salkind, 2003) and generalizability. Studies that focus on diametrically differing groups (Salkind, 2003) and demographics would also allow for further prospects for comparison and deeper understanding of the phenomenon of intuition in decision-making. In this sense, cultural differences might be a variable that affects the results. Additional factors that could be considered in future research include a wider range of decision-makers' personal and professional experience, job functions and responsibilities, skills and education. Further, research might prove useful if it met two criteria: (a) the exploration of the extent to which the findings gathered in this Delphi study are relevant to bank leaders of different gender; and (b) the feasibility of including the development of the intuitive ability in the behavioral training in banks. Moreover, studies that examine and compare the financial results between bank executives who make intuitive judgments and those who rely exclusively on rational thinking and numerical data might promote elucidation of the topic of intuition in decision-making.

Recommendations

Based on the agreement of the panelists that the increased level of complexities in decision-making correlates with a growing integration of intuition into logical decision-making, it behooves banking organizations to ensure that creative decision-making tools are explored and utilized. The escalating unpredictability of political, social, and environmental conditions creates considerable shifts in power and control (Ghering, 2007) influences financial projections and calculations. From this viewpoint, rapid and accurate decisions will equally require broader, evolutionary expansions, and investigations into the untapped intuitional capabilities of the human mind. In the same manner, as Emotional Intelligence was a breakthrough for organizational behavior, organizations that chose to neglect the intuitional component in decision-making, might be overlooking the prospect of revolutionizing their paradigms and thus precluding themselves from utilizing resources that might prove valuable.

Summary

Chapter 5 presented the conclusions, implications to leadership and recommendations drawn from the analysis of data described in chapter 4. Reflections into the ways in which the study generated additional knowledge on the topic of intuition in the decision-making patterns of bank leaders were offered. In particular, panelists' responses where evaluated in the context of the problem statement, in comparison with the information gleaned from the literature review and from recent studies on the topic of intuition. Findings from this Delphi study indicate that there appears to be a dearth in the bank leaders' comprehension of the concept of intuition. As a result, perceptions may be a factor in the use and acceptance of intuition as a genuine leadership decision-making tool. Further, panelists' indication of a significant use of intuition in decision-making seems to contradict the assertion that the rational approach to decisions supported by factual and numerical information is preferred to intuitive approaches.

Limitations inherent to the study such as instrument development and generalizability of results, which might have enhanced the study, were retrospectively examined. Additionally, unforeseen issues concerning time constraints, external to the administration of this study, and which limited the direction of the study were discussed. Possible implications and relevance of the study to the scientific field, to organizations, and to leadership in the banking industry were assessed as well. Recommendations for future research—of a constructive nature as well as those adopting a sterner outlook—were offered to the scientific community, to organizations, leaders, along with the supporting evidence from the literature review, and justification derived from the analyses and findings.

REFERENCES

Addis, M. and Podestà, S. (2005). Long life to marketing research: a postmodern view. *European Journal of Marketing, 39* (3/4), 386. Retrieved on June 2006 from the University of Phoenix ProQuest Database.

Adler, M., & Ziglio, E. (1996). *Gazing into the oracle.* Bristol, PA: Jessica Kingsley Publishers.

Agor, W. H. (1968). *The logic of intuitive decision-making. A research-based approach for top management.* Westport, Connecticut: Greenwood Press, Inc.

Agor, W. H. (1986). Intuition as a brain skill in management. *Public Personnel Management (14)*, 15-25. Retrieved September 2005 from the University of Phoenix EBSCO Database.

Agor, W. H. (1990). *Intuition in organizations: Leading and managing productively.* Newbury Park, CA: Sage Publications.

Ahmad, N. H. (2002). Financial crisis and non-performing loans: The case of Malaysian banks. *International Journal of Finance, 14*(2), 2257. Retrieved July 2006 from The University of Phoenix EBSCO Database.

Alessandri, T. M. (2002). A portfolio of decision processes: Rationality in capital investments under perceptions of risk and uncertainty. Dissertation AAT 3070815. Retrieved November 2005 from the University of Phoenix ProQuest Dissertations Database.

Anderson, A. (2000).Quantum physics, quantum consciousness, and the new science: An interview with Dr. Friedbert Karger from Max Planck Institute in Germany. *New Thought 83*(26-27). Retrieved June 2005 from http://website.com/alan/intuit.htm.

Anderson, O. (2005). The good in the right: A theory of intuition and intrinsic value. *The Review of Metaphysics, 58* (4), 873. Retrieved August 2006 from the University of Phoenix ProQuest Database.

Anderson, W. T. (1933). *Reality isn't what it used to be.* New York: Harper Collins.

Andrioff, J. L. (2005). Good direction for direction trustees. *Benefits Law Journal, 18*(3), 63. Retrieved February 2006 from the University of Phoenix ProQuest database.

Aranha, M. L. A and Martins, M. H. P. (2005). *Temas de filosofia*. São Paulo: Editora Moderna Ltda.

Aranha, M. L., and Martins, M. H. P. (2005). *Themes of philosophy*. São Paulo: Editora Moderna Ltda.

Armitage, L.A. (2004). Factors affecting the adjustment of Koreans studying in Australia.Master's Thesis. Retrieved June 2005 from http://www.dfat.gov.au/akf/laa_images/laa_chapter5.html

Arntz, W. Chasse, B. and Vicente M. (2005). *What the bleep do we know? Discovering the endless possibilities for altering your everyday reality.* Deerfield Beach, FL: Health Communications, Inc.

Ashar, H., & Lane-Maher, M. (2004). Success and spirituality in the new business Paradigm. *Journal of Management Inquiry, 13*(3), 249. Retrieved August 2006 from the University of Phoenix EBSCO Database.

AskOxford.com (2006). Oxford Dictionaries. Retrieved August 2006 from http://www.askoxford.com/concise_oed/view?view=uk

Atkinson, (2001). Online research tools. Retrieved February 2006 from http://www.phi.umd.edu/contact

Atlas.ti.com (2006). Qualitative software. Retrieved February 2006 from http://www.atlasti.com/

Baggini, J. and Stangroom, J. (2003). *What philosophers think.* London: Continuum.

Bakken, B.T. and Gilljam, M. (2003). Dynamic intuition in military command and control: Why it is important and how it should be developed. *Cognition, Technology & Work, 5*(3), 197. Retrieved August 2006 from the University of Phoenix ProQuest Database.

Balanced Score Card Institute (2006). Management terms. Retrieved February 2006 from http://www.balancedscorecard.org/basics/definitions.html

Banco Central do Brasil (2006). Balance sheet and income statement as of October 2005. Retrieved December 2006 from http://www.bb.com.br/portal/ri/eng/dce/dwn/FinanStat4Q06.pdf

Banco Itaú Holding Financeira S.A. (2006). Annual and Quarterly Reports. Retrieved December 2006 from http://ww13.itau.com.br/portalri/index.aspx?idioma=port

Bank of America (2004). Portrait of a bank. Bank of America 2004 annual report. Retrieved January, 2006 from http://media.corporate-ir.net/media_files/irol/71/71595/reports/2004_ar.pdf

Bank of America (2006). Annual report 2006. Retrieved December 2006 from http://media.corporate-ir.net/media_files/irol/71/71595/reports/2006_AR.pdf

Banerji, P. and Krishnan, V. R. (2000). Ethical preferences of transformational leaders: An empirical investigation. *Leadership and Organization Development Journal, 21*(8), 405. Retrieved February 2006 from the University of Phoenix ProQuest database.

Banker's Academy (2005). Problem solving and decision-making effective solutions to even the most difficult problems. Retrieved November 2005 from http://bankersacademy.com/overture/analysis.html?OVRAW=decision%20making&OV KEY=decision%20making&OVMTC=standard

Bargh, J. A., Chartrand, T. L. (1999). The unbearable automaticity of being. *American Psychologist 54*(7), 462-479. Retrieved March 2005 from the University of Phoenix EBSCO Database.

Barnard, C. (1942).The functions of the executive. In R. Frantz (2003) *Journal of Economic Psychology, 24* www- rohan.sdsu.edu/~frantz/HSimon.html

Bass, B. M. (1990). *Bass and Stogdil's handbook of leadership. Theory, research, and managerial applications.* (3rd. Ed.). New York: The Free Press.

Beekie, B. R. (2004). The relationship between emotional intelligence and sales performance: from intuition to research. Dissertation. ATT 3144778. Retrieved August 2006 from the University of Phoenix ProQuest Dissertations Database.

Belkaoui, A. (2002). The effect of multinationality on security analyst underreaction. *Journal of Business Finance and Accounting, 29*(9/10), 1355-1356. Retrieved August 2006 from the University of Phoenix EBSCO Database.

Bérgson, H. (1992). *Leçons d'esthétique. Leçons de morale, psychologie et métaphysique.* Paris, France: Presses Universitaires de France.

Bergson, H. (1992). *Lessons on esthetics. Lessons on moral, psychology and metaphysics.* Paris, France: Presses Universitaires de France.

Bernanke, B. S. (2005). The logic of monetary policy. *Vital Speeches of the Day 71*(6), 165. Retrieved on February 2005 from the University of Phoenix EBSCO Database.

Birkett, N. J. (1986). Selecting the number of responses for a Likert-type scale. Retrieved September, 2005 from http://www.amstat.org/sections/srms/Proceedings/papers/1986_091.pdf.

Blotnicky, K. (2002). You cannot take your intuition to the bank; [Final Edition]. *Standard.* Retrieved August 2006 from the University of Phoenix ProQuest Database.

Bloxham, E. and Borge, D. (2006). Risk management and the CFO: A risk or an opportunity? *Corporate Finance Review, 10* (5), 21. Retrieved August 2006 from the University Of Phoenix ProQuest Database.

Bolman, L. & Deal, T. (1991). Reframing organizations: *Artistry, choice and leadership.* San Francisco: Jossey Bass.

Bolton, B. (2005). Your career in today's enterprise. *Information Systems Management, 22*(1), 86. Retrieved August 2006 from the University of Phoenix ProQuest Database.

Boyd, L., Gupta, M. and Sussman, L. (2001). A new approach to strategy formulation: Opening the black box. *Journal of Education for Business, 76*(6), 338. Retrieved August 2006 from the University of Phoenix ProQuest Database.

Brockman, E. N., and Simmonds, P.G. (1997).Strategic-decision making: The influence of CEO experience and use of tacit knowledge. *Journal of Managerial Issues, 9*(4).Retrieved January 2005 from the University of Phoenix ProQuest Database.

Brown, R. B. (2003). Emotion and behavior: Exercises in emotional intelligence. *Journal of Management Education, 27*(1), 122. Retrieved September 2005 from the University of Phoenix ProQuest Database.

Burke, L. A., Miller, M. K. (1999). Taking the mystery out of intuitive decision-making. *Academy of Management Executive, 13*(4), 91. Retrieved February 2004 from the University of Phoenix EBSCO Database.

Burns, J. M. (1978). *Leadership.* New York: Harper & Row.

Campbell, M.K. (2000). Exploring the relationship between emotional intelligence, intuition and responsible risk-taking in organizations. Dissertation. *AAT 9997529.* Retrieved on January 2005 from the University of Phoenix ProQuest Database. Website: www.apollolibrary.com/Library/databases.

Capra, F. (1991). *The Tao of physics. An exploration of the parallels between modern physics and Eastern mysticism.* (3rd Edition). Boston: Shambhala Publications, Inc.

Cartwright, T. (2004). Feeling your way: Enhancing leadership through intuition. *Leadership in Action, 24*(2), 8. Retrieved August 2006 from the University of Phoenix ProQuest Database.

Catao, L., Kapur, S. (2006). Volatility and the debt-intolerance paradox. *IMF Staff Papers, 53*(2), 195. Retrieved August 2006 from the University of Phoenix ProQuest Database.

Catena, M. (2003). Essays on international economics: The tequila and caipirinha effects. Dissertation. ATT 3110811. Retrieved August 2006 from the University of Phoenix ProQuest Dissertations Database.

Chang, W. L., Chang, K. W.C., Hsin, J. Y. H. (2006). Analysis of financial performance by strategic groups of digital learning industry in Taiwan. *Journal of American Academy of Business Cambridge, 10*(1), 198. Retrieved from the University of Phoenix ProQuest Database.

Chauí, M. (2003). *Filosofia.* São Paulo: Editora Atica.

Chauí, M. (2003). *Philosophy.* São Paulo: Editora Atica.

Chia, R. (2001). Foundations of management knowledge: Assumptions and limitations. Retrieved March 2007 from http://www.ex.ac.uk/sobeinternal/research/ Discussion Papers Man/Man2001/Man 0104.pdf

Church, M. J. (2005). Intuition, leadership, and decision-making: A phenomenon. Dissertation AAT 3177390. Retrieved November 2005 from the University of Phoenix Dissertations Database.

Citibank (2006). Investor relations. Financial statements. Retrieved December 2006 from http://www.citigroup.com/citigroup/fin/data/k06c.pdf

Clayton, M. J. (1997). Delphi: a technique to harness expert opinion for critical decision making tasks in education. *Educational Psychology 17*(4), 373. Retrieved March, 2005 from the University of Phoenix Proquest Database.

Cleary, C, Packard, T., Armenakis, A. A, Bederan, A. G., et all (1992). The use of metaphors in organizational assessment and change; the role of metaphors in organizational change: Change agent and change target perspectives; don't struggle to scope those metaphors yet; metaphors to consult by. *Group and Organization 17*(3), 229. Retrieved August 2005 from the University of Phoenix ProQuest Database.

Cohen, A. (2003). A leap into the future. DVD on authentic leadership for the 21st Century. Retrieved October 2005 from www.andrewcohen.org.

Collaborative IRB Training Initiative (CITI) (2006). Course in the protection of human research subjects. Retrieved August, 2006 from https://www. citiprogram.org/members/courseandexam/moduletext.asp?strKeyID= A7180D71-33F2-4D91-8D70-13D501E2D711-1008769

Collins, J. (2001). Level 5 leadership. *Harvard Business Review, 79*(1), 66. Retrieved February 2006 from the University of Phoenix ProQuest database.

Collins, L. A., Smith, A. J. (2004). Understanding the new investors in people standards- Lessons from experience. *Personnel Review, 33*(5/6), 583. Retrieved February 7, 2006 from the University of Phoenix ProQuest database.

Collins, S., Duschl R., Millar R., Osborne J., and Ratcliffe M. (2001). What 'ideas-about- science' should be taught in school science? A Delphi study of the "expert" community. Paper presented at the Annual Conference of the National Association for research in Science teaching, Saint Louis. Retrieved March 2005 from http://www. kcl.ac,uk/depsta/education/publications/delphi.pdf

Coop, C. F. (2006). Balancing the balanced score card for a New Zealand mental health service. *Australian Health Review, 30*(2), 174. Retrieved August 2006 from the University of Phoenix ProQuest Database.

Cooper, R. K., and Sawaf, A. (1997). *Executive EQ. Emotional intelligence in leadership and organizations.* New York: Perigee Book.

Cooper, D. R. and Schindler, P. S. (2003). *Business research methods* (8th Ed.). New York: McGraw-Hill Higher Education.

Cottringer, W. (2004). Successful critical thinking for maximum results. Retrieved on October 29, 2004 from http://www.metrokc.gov/prepare/docs/EC_Critical%20Thinking.ppt#1

Covey, S. (1989). *The seven principles of effective leadership.* New York: Fireside.

Creswell, J. W. (2002). *Educational research: Planning, conducting, and evaluating quantitative and qualitative research.* Upper Saddle River, NJ: Pearson Education Inc.

Daake, D., Dawley, D.D., Anthony, W. P. (2004). Formal data use in strategic planning: An organizational field experiment. *Journal of Managerial Issues, 16(2), 232.* Retrieved August 2006 from the University of Phoenix ProQuest Database.

Dalkey, N.D. (1969). *The Delphi Method: An experimental study of group opinion.* Santa Monica, CA: The RAND Corporation.

Dane, E., and Pratt, M.G. (2004). Intuition: Its boundaries and roles in organizational decision-making. *Academy of Management.* Retrieved on February 2, 2005 from the University of Phoenix EBSCO Database.

De Vet E., Brug J., De Nooijer J., Dijkstra A., and De Vries N. K. (2005). Determinants of forward stage transitions: a Delphi study. Health Education Research, 20(2), 195.Retrieved August 2006 from the University of Phoenix ProQuest Database.

Delbecq, A. L. (1975). *Group techniques for program planning. A guide to nominal and Delphi processes.* Glenville, Ill: Scott, Foresman and Company.

Department of Health, Education, and Welfare (1979). The Belmont report. Office of the secretary. Ethical principles and guidelines for the protection of human subjects of research. The National Commission for the Protection of Human Subjects of Biomedical and Behavioral Research. Retrieved August 2006 from http://www.hhs.gov/ohrp/humansubjects/guidance/Belmont.htm

Dick, B. (2000) *Delphi face to face* [On line]. Retrieved February 2007 from the Website: http://www.scu.edu.au/schools/gcm/ar/arp/delphi.html

Dwight, L.W. (2005). Essays in international banking and finance. Dissertation. ATT 3190817. Retrieved August 2006 from the University of Phoenix ProQuest Dissertations Database.

English, G. C. (2004). *Managing information and human performance: Strategies and methods for knowing your workforce and organization.* Amherst, Mass: HRD Press, Inc.

Eisenhardt, K.M. (1989). Making strategic decisions in high-velocity environments. *Academy of Management Journal, 32*(3), 543. Retrieved on February 2005 from the University of Phoenix EBSCO Database.

Familoni, O. J. (2002). Intuition, the hidden intelligence: Factors that influence intuition in decision-making of leaders from Nigeria and the United States. Dissertation. Retrieved October 28, 2004 from the University of Phoenix ProQuest Database. Website: www.apollolibrary.com/Library/databases.

Faugier, J. (2005). Basic instincts. *Nursing Standard, 19*(24), 14. Retrieved February 2006 from the University of Phoenix ProQuest Database.

Fisher, Fred. A. (1999). Intuitive leadership spirituality and business intuition. (Doctoral Dissertation Submitted to Spalding University, 1999). Publication number AAT 9962310. Retrieved on November 3, 2003 from the Spalding University Website: http://www.spalding.edu/library/dBases/dbdscrp.htm

Fowles, J., (1978). *Handbook of futures research.* Greenwood Press: Connecticut. *Journal of Economic Psychology, 24, 265-277.* www-rohan.sdsu.edu/~frantz/HSimon.html

Fulmer, R. M. (1994). A model for changing the way organizations learn. *Planning Review, 22*(3), 20-24. Retrieved May 2005 from the University of Phoenix ProQuest Database.

Gall, M.D., Borg, W., & Gall, J.P. (2003). *Educational research: An introduction.* (7th Ed.). New York: Longmans.

Gandossy, R. and Sonnenfeld, J. (2004). *Leadership governance from the inside out.* New Jersey: John Wiley and Sons.

Garfield, M. J., Taylor, N. J., Dennis, A. R., and Satzinger, J. W. (2001). Research report: Modifying paradigms - individual differences, creativity techniques, and exposure to ideas in-group idea generation. *Information Systems Research, 2*(3), 322. Retrieved February 6 2006 from the University of Phoenix ProQuest database.

Garmston, R. (2006). What groups talk about matters – and how they talk matters too. *Oxford, 27*(1), 73. Retrieved June 2006 from the University of Phoenix ProQuest Database.

Gaspar, M. and Napolitano, G. (2007). Gênios do mercado. *Revista Exame, 886*(2).

Gaspar, M. and Napolitano, G. (2007). Market geniuses. Exame Magazine, 886 (2).

Gehrman, E. (2002). Rubin eyes globalization and poverty: Former treasury secretary delivers conference keynote. Retrieved December 2005 from http://www.news.harvard.edu/gazette/2002/04.18/01-rubin.html

Ghering, V. V. (2007). The ethical dimensions of global development. *Reference and Research and Book News, 2*(1). Retrieved February 2007 from the University of Phoenix ProQuest database.

Gilsford, J.W. (1986-1998). Written corporate policy on communicating: A Delphi survey. *Management Communication Quarterly, 5*(3), 316. Retrieved February 14, 2006 from the University of Phoenix ProQuest database.

Gladwell, M. (2005). *Blink: The tipping point.* London: Penguin Books.

Goldberg, E. (2005). The wisdom paradox: How your mind can grow stronger as your brain grows older. New York: Gotham Books.

Goleman, D. (1996). *Emotional intelligence–Why it can matter more than IQ.* London: Bloomsbury Publishing.

Goleman, D. (1996). *Working with emotional intelligence.* New York: Batam Books.

Gomes, L.F. A. M., Gomes, C. F. S., and Almeida, A. T. (2002). *Tomada de decisão gerencial. Enfoque Multicriterio.* São Paulo: Editora Atlas.

Gomes, L.F. A. M., Gomes, C. F. S., and Almeida, A. T. (2002). *Management decision making. Multi-criteria focus.* São Paulo: Editora Atlas.

Graber, D.R. (2001). Spirituality and healthcare organizations. *Journal of Healthcare Management 46*(1), 39-50. Retrieved May 2005 from the University of Phoenix ProQuest database.

Greenleaf, R. K. (2002). What is servant leadership? The Greenleaf Center of Servant Leadership. Retrieved February 2006 from http://www.greenleaf.org/ leadership/servant-leadership/What-is-Servant- Leadership.html

Gregoriou, G. Messier, J., Sedzro, K. (2004). Assessing the relative efficiency of credit union branches using data envelopment analysis. Infor, 42(4), 281. Retrieved August 2006 from the University of Phoenix Database.

Griffin, D, and Kahneman, D. (2003). Judgmental heuristics: Human strengths or human weaknesses? *In: A psychology of human strengths: Fundamental questions and future directions for a positive psychology.* Aspinwall, L.G., and Staudinger, U. M. Washington, DC, US: American Psychological Association, 2003, pp. 165- 178.

Halpern, S. (2005). The moment of truth? *The New York Review of Books 52*(7). Retrieved November, 2005 form http://www.nybooks.com/articles/17954

Harper, D. (2001). Online Etymology Dictionary. Retrieved August 2006 from http:// www.etymonline.com/index.php?search=intuition&searchmode=none

Harrington, W.J., Preziosi, R. C., D. J. Gooden (2001). Perceptions of workplace spirituality among professionals and executives. *Employee Responsibilities and Rights Journal 13*(3), 155. Retrieved on June1, 2005 from the University of Phoenix ProQuest Database.

Harrison, B. (1999). The nature of leadership: Historical perspectives & the future. *Journal of California Law Enforcement, 33*(1), 24-30. Retrieved on June1, 2005 from the University of Phoenix ProQuest Database.

Hartman, F. T., and Baldwin A. (1995). Using technology to improve Delphi method. *Journal of Computing in Civil Engineering 9*(4), 244-249. Retrieved March, 2005 From http://www.pubs.asce.org/WWWdisplay.cgi?9505259

Hasson, F., Keeny, S., and McKeena, H. (2000). Research guidelines for the Delphi survey technique. *Journal of Advanced Nursing 32*(4). Retrieved November 2005 from the University of Phoenix ProQuest Database.

Hayashi, A. (2001). When to trust your gut. *Harvard Business Review 79*(2). Retrieved June 2005 from the University of Phoenix ProQuest Database.

Hayes, J. Allinson, C. W., and Armstrong, S. J. (2004). Intuition, women managers and gendered stereotypes. *Personnel Review 33*(4), 403. Retrieved September 2005 from the University of Phoenix ProQuest Database.

Heaton, D. P., Schmidt-Wilk, J., Travis, F. (2004). Constructs, methods, and measures for researching spirituality in organizations. *Journal of Organizational Change Management 17*(1), 62. Retrieved on March 1, 2005 from the University of Phoenix ProQuest Database.

Helmer, O. (1967). *Analysis of the future: The Delphi method*. Santa Monica, CA: The RAND Corporation.

Higgs, M. (2001). Is there a relationship between the Myers-Briggs type indicator and emotional intelligence? *Journal of Managerial Psychology, 16*(7/8), 509. Retrieved August 2006 from the University of Phoenix ProQuest Database.

Hillson, D. and Murray-Webster, R. (2004). Understanding and managing risk attitude. Retrieved February 7. 2006 from http://www.kent.ac.uk/scarr/events/finalpapers/Hillson%20+%20Murray- Webster.pdf

Homer, C and Westcott (2005). Thinking through philosophy. Massachusetts: Cambridge University Press.

Houston, P. D. and Sokolow, S. L. (2006). *The spiritual dimension of leadership. The 8 key principles of leading more effectively*. Boston: MA: Sage Publications.

Hsiao, C. (2003). *Analysis of panel data* (2nd Ed.). NY: Cambridge University Press.

Huges, P. J., Lang, W.W., Mester, J.L., Moon, C.G., & Pagano, M.S. (2003). Do bankers sacrifice value to build empires? Managerial incentives, industry consolidations and financial performance. *Journal of Banking and Finance 27*(3), 417. Retrieved August 2006 from the University of Phoenix EBSCO Database.

Illinois Institute of Technology. (2005). The Delphi method. Retrieved October 2005 from http://www.iit.edu/~it/delphi.html

Institute of International Finance, Inc. (2005). The global association of financial institutions. Retrieved September 2005 from http://www.iif.com/

Isenberg, D. (1984). How senior managers think? *Harvard Business Review, 81*(90). Retrieved August 2006 from the University of Phoenix ProQuest Database.

Jacobsen, M. (2005). Complementary research methods. Retrieved February 13, 2006, from http://www.ucalgary.ca/~dmjacobs/phd/methods/index.htm

Jankowski, P.J. (2002). Postmodern spirituality: Implications for promoting change. *Counseling and Values 47*(1), 69. Retrieved on March 1, 2005 from the University of Phoenix ProQuest Database.

Jefferey, D., Ley, A., Bennun, I., and McLaren, S. (2000). *Journal of Mental Health, 9* .

Jentz, B. C. and Murphy, J. T. (2005). Embracing confusion: What leaders do when they don't know what to do. *Phi Delta Kappan 86*(5), 358. Retrieved on February 10 from the University of Phoenix ProQuest Database.

Jung, C. G. (1973). *Synchronicity: an acausal connecting principle* (2nd Ed.). Princeton, N.J.: Princeton University Press.

Kay, J. (2002). *Financial Times, 9.* Retrieved August 2006 from the University of Phoenix ProQuest Database.

Kazlev, M.A. (2004). The four ego functions. Jung's psychological theory of types. The four ego faculties. Retrieved on February 2, 2005 from http://www.kheper.net/topics/Jung/typology.html

Keegan, W. (1984). *Judgments, choices and decisions. Effective management through self-knowledge.* New York: John Wiley and Sons.

Khatri, N. & Ng, H.A. (2000). The role of intuition in strategic decision-making. *Human Relations 53*(1), 57. Retrieved on November 2, 2003 from the University of Phoenix ProQuest Database.

Khatri, N., Ng, H.A., Lee, T. H. (2001). The distinction between charisma and vision: An empirical study. *Asia Pacific Journal of Management, 18*(3), 373. Retrieved August 2006 from the University of Phoenix ProQuest Database.

Kopeikina, L. (2006). The elements of a clear decision. *MIT Sloan Management Review, 47*(2), 19. Retrieved August 2006 from the University of Phoenix ProQuest Database.

Korac- Kakabadse, N., Kakabadse, A., and Kouzmin, A. (2002). Spirituality and leadership Praxis. *Journal of Managerial Psychology, 17*(3), 165. Retrieved on January 31, 2005 from the University of Phoenix ProQuest Database.

Korac-Kakabadse, N., Kakabadse, A., and Kouzmin, A. (2003). Reviewing the knowledge management literature: Towards a taxonomy. *Journal of Knowledge Management, 7*(4), 75. Retrieved on January 2005 from the University of Phoenix ProQuest Database.

Koretz, G. (2000). Women in the boardroom: Why their presence can be a plus. *Business Week, 3700* (30). Retrieved July 31, 2004 from ProQuest Database.

Korn Ferry International Management Survey Report (2001). Korn Ferry International Headquarters. Los Angeles: Korn Ferry.

Krishnan, R. (2001). Value systems of transformational leaders. *Leadership and Organization Development 22*(3). Retrieved on May, 2004 from the University of Phoenix ProQuest Database.

Kumar, R. and Dempsey, M. (2002). Kundalini, soul, and the right side of the brain. *Journal of Religion and Psychical Research, 25*(3), 148. Retrieved August 2006 from the University of Phoenix EBSCO Database.

Kutschera, I. (2002). Cognitive style and decision-making: implications of intuitive and analytical information processing for decision-making. Dissertation. ATT 3061952. Retrieved on February 2005 from the University of Phoenix ProQuest Dissertations Database.

Latham J &Vinyard, J. (2003). Baldrige user's guide to organization diagnosis, design, and transformation. New Jersey: John Wiley and Sons, Inc.

Law, J. and Owe, G. (Eds.) (1999). *A dictionary of accounting.* Oxford University Press. Oxford Reference Online. Retrieved August 2006 from the University of Phoenix Library: http://www. oxfordreference.com/views/ENTRY.html?subvie w=Main&entry=t17.e423.

Leedy, P. D. and Omrod, J.E. (2001). *Practical research: Planning and design* (7th Ed.). Upper Saddle River, NJ: Prentice Hall.

Leidner, D. E., Elam, J. J (1993-1994). Executive information systems: Their impact on executive decision-making. *Journal of Management Information Systems10* (3), 139. Retrieved on February 2, 2005 from the University of Phoenix EBSCO Database.

Leonard, N. H., Beauvais, L. L. and Scholl, R. W. (2005). A multi-level model of group cognitive style in strategic decision-making. *Journal of Managerial Issues, 17*(1), 119. Retrieved September 2005 from the University of Phoenix ProQuest Database.

Lewis, J. (2002). Binding the dichotomy: A reconciliation of opposites. *A Journal of Undergraduate Writing at Virginia Tech (4).* Retrieved June 2005 from http:// www.athena.english.vt.edu/~exlibris/essays02/lewis.html.

Linder, C. (2003). Economic forecasts said to be flawed. *American Banker 168*(239), 21. Retrieved February 2005 from the University of Phoenix EBSCO Database.

Linstone, H. A. and Turoff, M. (ed.) (2002). *The Delphi method: Techniques and applications.* MA: Addison-Wesley Publishing.

Lips-Wiersma, M. (2002). Analyzing the career concerns of spiritually oriented people: Lessons for contemporary organizations. *Career Development International, 7* (6/7), 385. Retrieved on February 2005 from the University of Phoenix ProQuest Database.

Liu, W. (2005). When intuition and deliberation converge: Two routes to the default option. Retrieved November, 2005 from the Stanford University Website: http://pages.stern.nyu.edu/~mkt/Seminar%20Series/WendyLiu/ WendyLiuCVSept ember2 005.pdf

Lloyd, B. and Mori, M. (2002). Leadership. An "alternative view". *Leadership and Organizational Development Journal, 23*(3/4), 228. Retrieved August 2006 from the University of Phoenix ProQuest Database.

Ludwig, B. (1997). Predicting the Future: Have you considered using the Delphi Methodology? *Journal of Extension 35*(5). Retrieved June, 2005 from http://www.joe.org/joe/1997october/tt2.html.

Mann, D. K. M. (1997). A comparison of the issues in special education in Victoria, Australia and Nebraska, United States of America. Dissertation. UMI 9805514. Retrieved September 2005 from the University of Phoenix ProQuest Database.

Marques, J. (2005). Yearning for a more spiritual workplace. *Journal of American Academy of Business, Cambridge, 7*(1), 149. Retrieved August 2006 from the University of Phoenix ProQuest Database.

Marques, J. (2005). Socializing a capitalistic world: Redefining the bottom line. *Journal of American Academy of Business 7*(1), 283. Retrieved February, 2005 from the University of Phoenix ProQuest Database.

Martino, J.P. (1978).The log normality of Delphi estimates. *Technological Forecasting 1*(4), 355-58. Retrieved September 2005 from the University of Phoenix ProQuest Database.

McCraty, R., Atkinson, M., and Bradley, R. T. (2004). Electrophysiological evidence of intuition. Part 2: A system-wide process? *Journal of Alternative and Complementary Medicine, 10*(2), 325-336. Retrieved August 2006 from the University of Phoenix EBSCO Database.

McLean, J. (2005). Management and leadership dispelling the myths. *The British Journal of Administrative Management* 16. Retrieved November 2005 from the University of Phoenix ProQuest Database.

McMackin, J., and Slovic, P. (2000). When does explicit justification impair decision-making? *Applied Cognitive Psychology, 14*(6), 527-541. Retrieved August 2006 from the University of Phoenix EBSCO Database.

McNaughton, R. D. (2003). The use of meditation and intuition in decision-making: Reports from executive meditators. Dissertation. *AAT 3093260*. Retrieved on January 2005 from the University of Phoenix ProQuest Database. Website: www.apollolibrary.com/Library/databases.

Medina, J. and Wood, D. (2005). *Truth: Engagements from philosophical traditions.* New York: Blackwell Publishing.

Michaud, S. (2002). The influence of information processing style on decision-making Effectiveness. Dissertation. DAÍ-B 63, 07. Retrieved November 2003 from the University of Phoenix ProQuest Dissertations Database.

Miller, C. C. and Ireland, R.D. (2005). Intuition in strategic decision-making: Friend or foe in the fast-paced 21 century? *Academy of Management Executive, 19*(1). Retrieved February 2005 from the University of Phoenix EBSCO Database.

Mintzberg, H. (1994). The rise and fall of strategic planning: Reconceiving roles for planning, *plans, planners.* London: Pearson Professional Education.

Mishlove, J. (1994). Intuition: the true source of knowing. *Noetic Sciences Review 29.* Retrieved April 2005 from the University of Phoenix EBSCOhost Database. Website: www.apollolibrary.com/Library/databases.

Mitroff, I. I (2004). William James and a theory of thinking. *JITTA: Journal of Information Technology Theory and Application, 6*(2), 83. Retrieved August 2006 from the University of Phoenix ProQuest Database.

Moser, P. K. and vander Nat, A. (2003). Human knowledge. Classical and contemporary approaches. (3rd Ed.). New York: Oxford University Press.

Mullen, P. (2003). Delphi: Myths and reality. *Journal of Organizational Health and Management 17*(1), 37. Retrieved June 2005 from the University of Phoenix ProQuest Database.

Myers, D. (2002). Intuition: *Its perils and power.* Yale: University Press.

Nassar, D. T. (2006). Immediacy and mediation in Schleiermacher's reden uber die religion. *The Review of Metaphysics, 59*(4), 807. Retrieved August 2006 from the University of Phoenix ProQuest Database.

Neurondorfer, B. and Hilz M. J. (1997). Ludwig Muller "a pioneer in autonomic nervous system research". *Clinical Autonomic Research Journal, 8,* 1. Retrieved February 2007 from SpringerLink Science and Business Media. **Department of Neurology, University of Erlangen-Nuremberg, Schwabachanlage 6, D-91054 Erlangen, Germany.** http://www.springerlink.com/content/ t46685927r551277/

Neuman W. L. (1997). *Social research methods. Qualitative and quantitative approaches.* (3rd Ed.). Boston: Allyn and Bacon.

Neuman W. L. (2000). *Social research methods. Qualitative and quantitative approaches.* (4th Ed.). Boston: Allyn and Bacon.

Olshfiski, D. and Joseph, A. (1991). Assessing training needs of executives using the Delphi technique. *Public Productivity and Management Review, 14* (3), 297-301. Retrieved June 2006 from the University of Phoenix ProQuest Database.

Orcher, L.T. (2005). *Social and behavioral science methods.* Glendale, CA: Pyrczak Publishers.

Owen, D. (2002). *Hume's reason*. Retrieved February 2005 from the University of
　　Phoenix Oxford Scholarship Online Database.

Oxford English Dictionary (2006). Oxford University Press's dictionary online.
　　Retrieved August 2006 from www.oed.com

Pablo, A. L. (1999). Managerial risk interpretation: Does industry make a difference?
　　Journal of Managerial Psychology, 14(12). Retrieved February 2005 from the
　　University of Phoenix EBSCO Database.

Papineau, D. (2002). *Thinking about consciousness*. London: King's College. Retrieved
　　February 2005 from the University of Phoenix Oxford Scholarship Online
　　Database.

Parikh, J., Neubauer, F, and Lank, A. G. (1994). *Intuição, a nova fronteira da
　　administração*. São Paulo: Editora Cultrix.

Parikh, J., Neubauer, F, and Lank, A. G. (1994). *Intuition, the new business frontier*. São
　　Paulo: Editora Cultrix.

Patton, M. Q. (2001). *Qualitative research and evaluation methods* (3rd Ed.). Thousand
　　Oaks, CA: Sage Publications.

Patton, J.R. (2003). Intuition in decisions. *Journal of Management Decision, 41*(9), 989-
　　996. Retrieved on January 2005 from the University of Phoenix Emerald Group
　　Publishing Limited.

Perkel, S. E. (2004). Primal leadership: Realizing the power of emotional intelligence.
　　Consulting to Management 15(3), 56. Retrieved June, 2005 from the University
　　of Phoenix ProQuest Database.

Philippe, M. (2002). *Introdução à filosofia de Aristóteles*. São Paulo: Paulus.

Philippe, M. (2002). *Introduction to Aristotle's philosophy*. São Paulo: Paulus.

Pietroski, P.M. (2002). *Causing actions*. Retrieved February 2005 from the University
　　of Phoenix Oxford Scholarship Online Database.

Pluhar, W. S. (1999). *Emmanuel Kant: The critique of pure reason*. Indianapolis: Hackett
　　Publishing.

Pope, A. (2005). The roots of sound rational thinking. Retrieved May 2005 from
　　http://www.plusroot.com/dbook/05intuition.html

Porth, S. (2003). Religion, spirituality, and decision-making: A preliminary
　　investigation. Retrieved on November 5, 2003 from the Website: http://www.
　　stthomas.edu/cathstudies/cstm/antwerp/p27.htm

Pounds, W. F. (2006). Why do good? *MIT Sloan Management Review, 47*(3), 14.
　　Retrieved June 2006 from the University of Phoenix ProQuest Database.

Rappaille, C. (2006). Marketing to the reptilian brain. *Forbes, 178* (1), 44. Retrieved February 2007 from the University of Phoenix EBSCO Database.

Rappaport, A. (2006). 10 ways to create shareholder value. *Harvard Business Review, 84*(9), 66-77. Retrieved August 2006 from the University of Phoenix EBSCO Database.

Ratcliffe, M. (1999) Evaluation of abilities in interpreting media reports of scientific research. *International Journal of Science Education 21*(10). 1085-1099. Retrieved May 2005 from http://www.york.ac.uk/depts/educ/projs/HPST2001

Reale, G. (2005). *Aristóteles. Metafísica.* São Paulo: Edições Loyola.

Reale, G. (2005). *Aristotle. Methaphysics. Sao Paulo: Loyola.*

Reimer, B. (2004). New brain research on emotion and feeling. Dramatic implications for music education. *Arts Education Policy Review 106*(2), 21. Retrieved September 2005 from the University of Phoenix ProQuest Database.

Rockwell, K., Furgason, J., Marx, D. B. (2000). Research and Evaluation Needs for Distance Education: A Delphi Study. Retrieved February 7, 2006 from http://www.westga.edu/~distance/ojdla/fall33/rockwell33.html

Rodriguez, C., Kergoat, M., Latour J., Lebel, P., and Contandriopoulos, A. (2003). Admission criteria in short-term geriatric assessment units: A Delphi study. *Canadian Journal of Public Health, 94*(4), 310. Retrieved August 2006 from the University of Phoenix ProQuest Database.

Rogers, P. and Wiseman, R. (2005/2006). Self-perceived high intuitiveness: An initial exploration. *Imagination, Cognition, and Personality, 25*(2), 161. Retrieved March 2007 from the University of Phoenix ProQuest Database.

Rorrer, A. K., and Skrla, L. (2005). Leaders as policy mediators: The reconceptualization of accountability. *Theory into Practice 44*(1), 53. Retrieved February 2005 from the University of Phoenix ProQuest Database.

Rowan, R. (1986). *Gerente por Intuição.* Rio de Janeiro: Editora Record.

Rowan, R. (1986). *Managing by intuition.* Rio de Janeiro: Editora Record.

Rowe, H.I. (2005). Collaborative Delphi. Retrieved June, 2005 from http://sustainablerangelands.warnercnr.colostate.edu/Meetings/Conferences/symposium%20proceedings/rowe.pdf.

Sadler-Smith, E., and Shefy, E. (2004). The intuitive executive: Understanding and applying "gut feel" in decision-making. *The Academy of Management Executive, 18*(4). Retrieved January 2006 from the University of Phoenix ProQuest Database.

Sanders III, J.E., Geroy, G.D. & Hopkins, W.E. (Spring 2003). From transactional to transcendental: Toward an integrated view of leadership. *Journal of Leadership & Organizational Studies, 9*(4), 21. Retrieved February 2005 from the University of Phoenix ProQuest Database.

Salkind, N.J. (2003). *Exploring research.* (Fifth Edition). Upper Saddle River: New Jersey: Pearson Education International.

San Francisco Estuary Institute (2001).Final Pilot/Special Study Selection Procedure. Retrieved June, 2005 from http://www.sfei.org/rmp/documentation/study_selection/FinalSelect_pilotspecial. html

Schmidt, V. V. (1995). Awakening intuition: A Delphi study. Dissertation 9543808. Retrieved February 2005 from the University of Phoenix ProQuest Dissertations Database.

Scholl, W., Konig, C., Meyer, B. and Heisig, P. (2004). The future knowledge management: an international Delphi study. *Journal of Knowledge Management, 8*(2), 19. Retrieved June 2005 from the University of Phoenix ProQuest Database.

Schurmans, F. Mavaddat, M. (2004). The golden rules of a successful merger. *Credit Union Management 27*(12), 8. Retrieved on February 2, 2005 from the University of Phoenix EBSCO Database.

Simões, L.M. (). *Es repetidor ou criador? Para jovens e adolescentes.* Editorial Angelorum Novalis.

Simões, L.M. (). Are you a copier or a creator? To youngsters and adolescents. Editorial Angelorum Novalis.

Simon, H. A. (1947). *Administrative Behavior: A study of decision-making processes in administrative organization.* New York: Macmillan Co.

Simon, M. K. (2006). *Qualitative research. The "l" side in the paradigm war.* Paper presented at University of Phoenix, AZ.

Slater, C. (2005). The evolution of credit risk management. *Credit Management, 38.* Retrieved July 2006 from the University of Phoenix EBSCO Database.

Sowerby, D. F. (2001). The light of inner guidance: A heuristic study of the recognition and interpretation of intuition. Doctoral dissertation, Institute of Transpersonal Psychology, Palo Alto. Retrieved June 2005 from the University of Phoenix ProQuest Database.

Standard & Poors (2005). Credit ratings news. Retrieved October 2005 from http://www2.standardandpoors.com/servlet/Satellite?pagename=sp/Page/HomePg & r=1&l=EN&b=10

Standards for Educational and Psychological Testing (1985). American Psychological Association Washington D.C.: AERA Publications.

Starratt, R. J. (2005). Responsible leadership. *The Educational Forum 69*(2), 124. Retrieved February 2005 from the University of Phoenix ProQuest Database.

Stuter, L. (1998). Using the Delphi technique to achieve consensus. *Education Reporter, 154*. Retrieved March, 2007 from http://www.eagleforum.org/educate/1998/nov98/focus.html

Symonds, C. L. (2005). Days of glory: The army of Cumberland, 1861-1865. *The Journal of Military History, 69*(1), 237. Retrieved February 2005 from the University of Phoenix ProQuest Database.

Tal, D. (2004). Between intuition and professionalism: Israeli military leadership during the 1948 Palestine war. *The Journal of Military History, 68*(3), 885. Retrieved August 2006 from the University of Phoenix ProQuest Database.

Taylor, S. & Bogdan, R. (1998). *Introduction to qualitative research methods. A guidebook and resource* (3 rd Ed.). New York: Springer.

The Bhagavad-Gita Trust. (2004). Retrieved on March 14, 2004 from the Website: http://www.bhagavad-gita.org/

The Cambridge Dictionary Online (2005). Retrieved December 2005 from the Cambridge University Press website: http://dictionary.cambridge.org/results.asp?searchword=views

The Idea Bridge (2002). The Idea Bridge paper series. Retrieved May, 2005 from http://www.ideabridge.com/ideabridgecom/whitepapers/64.pdf

The Institute of International Finance Inc. (2005). Emerging market research. Retrieved October 2005 from http://www.iif.com

The Merriam-Webster's Collegiate Dictionary (2006). In The Encyclopaedia Britannica Online (2006). Retrieved February 2006 from the University of Phoenix Library. *Tischler*, L., *Biberman*, J., and *McKeage*, R. (2002). *Journal of Managerial Psychology, 17* 203. Retrieved August 2004 from ProQuest Database.

Tollefsen, D. P. (2002). Interpreting organizations. Dissertation. ATT 3049124. Retrieved August 2006 from the University of Phoenix Dissertations ProQuest Database.

Topper, W.W. (2006). Leadership change in privately controlled businesses: A Delphi study of succession planning best practices. Dissertation. UMI 3206379. Retrieved July 2006 from the University of Phoenix ProQuest Dissertations Database.

Trailer, J. W., and Morgan, J. F. (2004). Making "good" decisions: What intuitive physics reveal about the failure of intuition. *Journal of American Academy of Business, Cambridge, 4* (1/2), 42. Retrieved August 2006 from the University of Phoenix ProQuest database.

Tubbs, S. L. and Schulz, E. (2006). Exploring taxonomy of global leadership competencies and meta-competencies. *Journal of American Academy of Business, 8*(2), 29. Retrieved January 2006 from the University of Phoenix ProQuest database.

Tuttle, W.W. (1988). The role of intuition in education (Buddhism). Dissertation. AAT 8902302. Retrieved on August 29, 2003 from ProQuest Dissertations Database. University of South Dakota (2004). Qualitative dissertation framework. Retrieved November 2005 from the University of South Dakota Website: http://www.usd.edu/ahed/qualguide.cfm

Uhlman, K. L. (2006). Corporate transformations and collaborative partnerships in mission critical facilities: A Delphi study. Dissertation. AAT 3220547. Retrieved February 2007 from the University of Phoenix Dissertation Database.

Vaill, P.B. (1996). *Learning as away of being: Strategies for survival in a world of permanent white water.* San Francisco, CA: Jossey-Bass.

Vaaler, P.M. and McNamara, G. (2004). Crisis and competition in expert organizational decision-making: Credit-rating agencies and their response to turbulence in emerging economies. *Organization Science, 15*(6), 687. Retrieved February 2006 from the University of Phoenix ProQuest database.

Watkins, S. S. (2004). Twenty-first-century corporate governance: The growing pressure on the board toward a corporate solution. In: Gandossy, R., and Sonnenfeld, J. *Leadership from the inside out* (pp. 27-36). New Jersey, Hoboken: John Wiley and Sons, Inc.

Webster's Online Dictionary (2001). Retrieved August 2006 from http://www.websters-online-dictionary.org/definition/attitude

Weiskittel, P. (1999). The concept of leadership. *ANNA Journal, 26*(5), 467. Retrieved February 7, 2006 from the University of Phoenix ProQuest database.

Wheatley, M. J. (1999). Leadership and the new science: Discovering order in a chaotic world. San Francisco: Berrett- Koehler.

Wren, D. A. (1994). *The evolution of management thought* (4th Ed.). Berkeley: John Wiley and Sons, Inc.

Wright, S. (2006). Does size matter? How many questions is too many? Retrieved June, 2006 from http://surveysurvival.2leadership.com/ssartsq11.htm

Xu, G., Gutierrez, J. A. (2006). An exploratory study of killer applications and critical success factors in M-Commerce. *Journal of Electronic Commerce in Organizations, 4* (3), 63. Retrieved August 2006 from the University of Phoenix ProQuest Database.

Yaghmaie, F. (2003). Content validity and its estimation. *Journal of Medical Education.* Retrieved June, 2005 from http://www.sbmu.ac.ir/Journal/MedEdu/jme7no1/ Content%20validity%20and%2 0it s%20estimation.htm

Yogananda, P. (2003). *The divine romance.* Los Angeles: Self-Realization Fellowship. Yogananda, P. (2003). *Man's eternal quest.* Los Angeles: Self-Realization Fellowship.

Zingano, M. (2005). Sobre a metafísica de Aristóteles. São Paulo: Odysseus.

Zingano, M. (2005). About Aristotle metaphysics. Sao Paulo: Odysseus.

Zoomerang.com. (2006). Online survey services. Retrieved August 2006 from http: info.zoomerang.com/

Zukav, G. (1991). *The seat of the soul.* New York: Fireside.

www.ingramcontent.com/pod-product-compliance
Lightning Source LLC
Chambersburg PA
CBHW081122170526
45165CB00008B/2521

* 9 7 8 1 4 3 4 3 7 9 0 6 1 *